THE BEST IN TENT CAMPING:

THE OZARKS

A Guide for Car Campers Who Hate RVs, Concrete Slabs, and Loud Portable Stereos

THE BEST IN TENT CAMPING:

THE OZARKS

A Guide for Car Campers Who Hate RVs, Concrete Slabs, and Loud Portable Stereos

Steve Henry

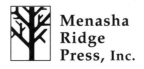

Menasha
Ridge
Press, Inc.

This book is for my family and friends. Your companionship and support is a blessing and an inspiration.

Printed in the United States of America
Published by Menasha Ridge Press
Distributed by The Globe Pequot Press
First edition, first printing

Library of Congress Cataloging-in-Publication Data

Henry, Steve.
    The best in tent camping, the Ozarks : a guide for car campers who hate RVs, concrete slabs, and loud portable stereos / by Steve Henry.—1st ed.
        p. cm.
    Includes bibliographical references and index.
    ISBN 0-89732-384-X
    1. Camp sites, facilities, etc.—Ozark Mountains—Guidebooks.
2. Camping—Ozark Mountains—Guidebooks.   3. Ozark Mountains—Guidebooks.   I. Title.
    GV199.42.O96 H45   2001
    917.67'10454—dc21

                                                                00-054905
                                                                CIP

Cover Design by Grant Tatum
Cover Photo by Dennis Coello
Maps by Raffaele De Gennaro

Menasha Ridge Press
P.O. Box 43673
Birmingham, AL 35243
www.menasharidge.com

CONTENTS

MAP LEGEND

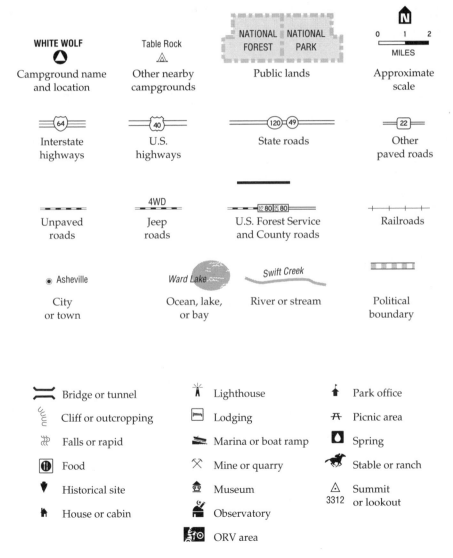

WHITE WOLF

Campground name
and location

Table Rock

Other nearby
campgrounds

NATIONAL FOREST   NATIONAL PARK

Public lands

0   1   2
MILES

Approximate
scale

64

Interstate
highways

40

U.S.
highways

120 49

State roads

22

Other
paved roads

Unpaved
roads

4WD

Jeep
roads

80 80

U.S. Forest Service
and County roads

Railroads

Asheville

City
or town

Ward Lake

Ocean, lake,
or bay

Swift Creek

River or stream

Political
boundary

Bridge or tunnel

Cliff or outcropping

Falls or rapid

Food

Historical site

House or cabin

Lighthouse

Lodging

Marina or boat ramp

Mine or quarry

Museum

Observatory

ORV area

Park office

Picnic area

Spring

Stable or ranch

3312 Summit
or lookout

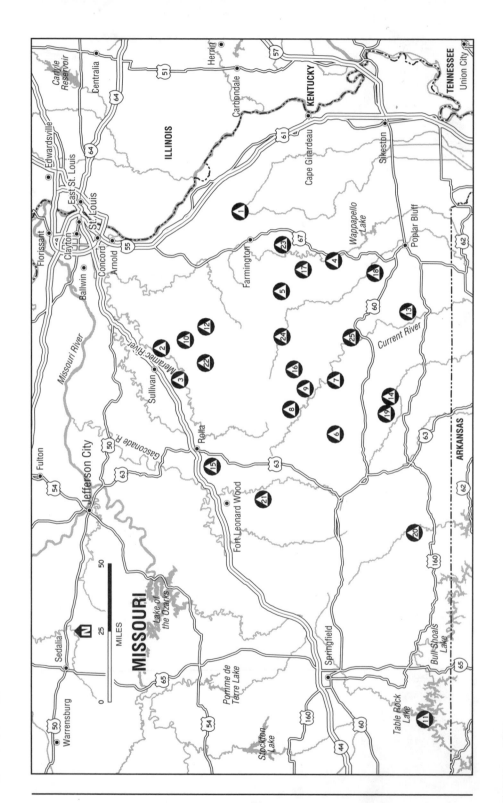

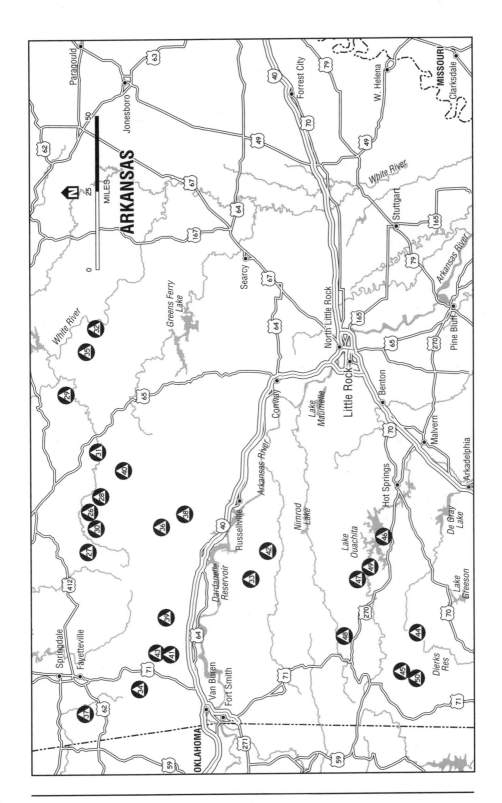

MISSOURI
Missouri State Parks
1. Hawn State Park
2. Meramec State Park
3. Onondaga Cave State Park
4. Sam A. Baker State Park
5. Taum Sauk Mountain State Park

Ozark National Scenic Riverways
6. Bay Creek
7. Powder Mill
8. Pulltite
9. Round Spring

Mark Twain National Forest
10. Berryman Trail
11. Big Bay
12. Council Bluffs
13. Deer Leap and Float Camp
    Recreation Areas
14. Greer Crossing
15. Lane Spring
16. Loggers Lake
17. Marble Creek
18. Markham Spring
19. McCormack Lake
20. North Fork
21. Paddy Creek
22. Red Bluff Recreation Area
23. Silver Mines
24. Sutton Bluff
25. Watercress Spring

ARKANSAS
Buffalo National River
26. Kyles Landing
27. Lost Valley
28. Ozark
29. Rush Landing
30. Steel Creek
31. Tyler Bend

Ozark National Forest
32. Blanchard Springs
33. Cove Lake
34. Devil's Den State Park
35. Gunner Pool
36. Haw Creek Falls
37. Lake Wedington
38. Long Pool
39. Redding
40. Richland Creek
41. Shores Lake
42. Spring Lake
43. White Rock Mountain

Ouachita National Forest
44. Albert Pike
45. Bard Springs
46. Charlton
47. Dragover
48. Mill Creek
49. River Bluff
50. Shady Lake

PREFACE

I had a blast cruising scenic and winding Ozark highways while researching these beautiful campgrounds. My only regret was not having time to spend several days in each one. Now that the book is finished, I can do what I hope is in the cards for you—spend several seasons checking out these wonderful hideaways in the Ozark Mountains. I've hiked or biked most trails mentioned in these chapters and paddled more than a few of the rivers. On my wanderings I've meandered along forested mountainsides, gazed awestruck from 500-foot bluffs, picnicked in rocky glades, explored spectacular caves, stared deep into aquamarine springs, and napped in meadows of wildflowers.

From these campgrounds you can also experience those Missouri and Arkansas backcountry pleasures. Thousands of miles of streams await your canoe, paddle, and fishing pole. These cool, spring-fed rivers and creeks are the perfect antidote to the heat and humidity of summer, and several of the sparkling-clear springs are among the largest in the world. All are accessible by car, canoe, or a short hike. When the weather cools, it's time to get out of the river and explore the rugged countryside on hundreds of miles of hiking and mountain biking trails.

Don't stop your camping exploration with these 50 campgrounds—many more scenic hideaways await you in the Ozarks. Nor should you let the off-season weather limit your camping season. You'll see better views from overlooks when the leaves are off the trees. Cooler temperatures also mean no bugs or crowded campgrounds. Winter skies offer incredible stargazing, and in December and January the remote mountains are perfect for enjoying two of the heavens' biggest meteor showers. I'll never forget winter camping next to a southwest Missouri creek, where ice columns three feet thick towered 100 feet over the streambed from an overlooking bluff. During winter, I'm thankful to live in the Midwest instead of the Rockies. When campgrounds and trails in those spectacular western mountains are choked with snow, I can still wander the Ozark hills.

Don't take my word for it—pick up this book and a couple of trail guides, round up some maps, toss your camping gear into the car, and head for the hills to see for yourself. Hope to see you out there!

—Steve Henry

THE BEST IN TENT CAMPING:

THE OZARKS

A Guide for Car Campers Who Hate RVs, Concrete Slabs, and Loud Portable Stereos

INTRODUCTION

A Word about This Book and Ozark Mountain Camping

Welcome to the rugged hills and hollows of the Ozark and Ouachita mountains, where you'll find some of the prettiest campgrounds in America. This is a land of clear rivers, tall bluffs, deep forests, and aquamarine springs. Hundreds of miles of trails and thousands of miles of rivers lace the countryside around these scenic forest camps, waiting for you to explore on hiking, biking, or paddling adventures.

Haunting reminders of the past will pique your interest in these Ozarks hideaways. Many of the campgrounds were built by the Civilian Conservation Corps (CCC) in the 1930s, and they showcase the unique native stone and wood architecture for which CCC projects are famous. Several of the campgrounds are actual sites of old CCC camps, where you can wander past crumbling foundations and chimneys from the long-gone work camps whose legacy we still enjoy 70 years later.

Other common remnants of old times in the Ozarks are the numerous mill sites scattered throughout the hills. It seems that every campground in the Ozarks once had a mill operating nearby. Nearly every stream or spring large enough to roll a water wheel once powered a mill to grind corn, saw logs, gin cotton, and card wool for the farmers working their hardscrabble Ozark farms. Some of these mills are gone without a trace. At others you can find remnants of the dams and raceways but little else. Several are still-standing, dilapidated ghosts, and a few, like Alley Mill and Dillard Mill, are restored historic structures. Once busy community centers, these mills are now quiet, visited only by hikers and the ghosts of their once-busy streamside communities.

All seasons are wonderful for camping in the Ozarks. Though summer is often hot and humid, the rivers, swimming holes, and lakes at most campgrounds keep campers comfortable in even the worst heat wave. Spring is a really wonderful time to be outdoors in the Ozarks—wildflowers are everywhere, dogwood and redwood blooms brighten the gray forest, turkeys gobble in the early morning, and spring peepers serenade you from the lakes and streams near camp. Fall is nearly everyone's favorite. Cold frosty mornings chip away at the lassitude left from summer's heat. In fall's crisp air you begin breathing easily and deeply for the first time in months, and your body wakes up ready to hit the trails. Pleasing hues of orange, red, yellow, and caramel decorate the forest as the trees prepare to shed their summer foliage. Next to fall, I really enjoy winter camping. The humidity, heat, bugs, and crowds are

---

gone, the streams are shallow and easier to cross, and the bare trees open up scenic views obscured by lush foliage during the warmer months.

The Rating System

These campgrounds are rated on a five-star system. A rating of five stars is wonderful, and one star is acceptable. Though these ratings are subjective, they're still excellent guidelines for finding the camping experience for you and your companions.

Beauty

All 50 campgrounds in this guide are wonderful places. In the Ozarks, the most beautiful campgrounds overlook one of the scenic rivers meandering through the forested hills, often with bluffs towering near the campsites. Others are on mountaintops. Even those without a five-star rating are comfortable hideaways that you'll hate to leave on hiking, canoeing, biking, or other explorations in the surrounding Ozarks Mountains.

Site Privacy

I'm really particular on this feature. For an outdoor misanthrope like me, few campgrounds have sites far enough apart. Campgrounds with good spacing and brushy growth between the sites offer the best seclusion, and many of the hideaways in this guide fill that bill. Some do not, but I included them because they were in beautiful settings or had lots of nearby outdoor activities to choose from. In general, you'll find that state parks offer the least privacy, and national forests offer the most.

Site Spaciousness

Some folks like open space around their campsite. Even if they have the most private site on the planet, they still feel crowded if their car, table, and tent are jammed too closely together. Others camp with friends and thus need room for two or three tents on their site. Camping spots rated high in this category are usually level sites with grassy open spaces surrounding them, often with a nice view of the adjacent countryside.

Quiet

This is another big one for me. Most of the campgrounds included here are far from roads, towns, railroads, and the like, so they're very peaceful. The wild card is you and your neighbors. In the hushed settings where you'll find these campgrounds, one loud group can ruin things for everyone. Avoid three-day summer weekends and nearby festivals and you'll almost always enjoy peace and quiet in these Ozark enclaves.

Security

Unless there's a heavy ranger or host presence, you need to watch your stuff no matter where you camp. Consequently, few campgrounds get a five-star rating. On the other hand, just one received less than four stars, and that was only because signs warning campers to lock their valuables were posted in the campground. Ozark campgrounds are usually as safe as they are beautiful, especially if you keep your camp buttoned up and neat while you are away enjoying the outdoors. And don't forget security from our four-legged and feathered friends, too. Keep a clean camp and you won't come home to a shambles made by marauding raccoons, squirrels, blue jays, and bears.

Cleanliness/Upkeep

Almost every campground in this guide rates five stars. Only a few do not, and they are usually the most remote and unvisited sites. These out-of-the-way campgrounds are very beautiful but just don't get as much attention from both campers and maintenance crews as their well-manicured brethren. They are often my favorites for that very reason. Overall, you'll be impressed with the clean and attractive appearance of these Ozark homes-away-from-home.

Both Missouri and Arkansas have beautiful and well-developed state park systems that are very worthy of a visit. Unfortunately, campsites in these state park campgrounds are packed cheek-to-cheek. They offer much less privacy than their national forest and national river counterparts and are more popular with RV and travel-trailer campers. Several state park campgrounds are included because those particular parks are too fascinating to be left out or their campgrounds are more laid-back than most. Missouri and Arkansas are blessed with three national forests and two national rivers containing thousands of peaceful campsites, and these are definitely better for tent camping than the campsites in most state parks.

Since I'm a winter camper, I wish all campgrounds stayed open year-round. Sadly, some of the most beautiful do not. Seasons stated in each chapter were current at the time this book was written. Beware of changes in seasons, fees, dates of water availability, and campground facilities. Campgrounds are constantly being improved, constructed, and, occasionally, closed. Especially dicey are water availability dates. At some year-round campgrounds, weather dictates when the water supply is turned on and off. When in doubt, call the agency operating the campground. That way you'll never be caught short.

To avoid crowds, I always invoke the three-day weekend rule—Just Say No to Camping on Memorial Day, July Fourth, or Labor Day weekends. At these times campgrounds are almost always full. Avoid weekends when a nearby special event might fill the campground you are considering. I've noted these when possible, but you just never know when you're going to stumble on the Rock and Roll Rappers Reunion Party and Campout at your chosen "getaway" site. But lucky you—if you have this book, you'll always be able to find a nice alternative, won't you? Camp during the week whenever possible, and you'll often have one of these Ozark hideaways all to yourself.

My most enjoyable camping experiences happen when I learn about and explore the countryside around my campground. To me, exploring a landscape without knowing about it is like reading a book in a foreign language—I can admire the pretty pictures, but I can't read the deeper and more fascinating story behind them. The information in this book, extensive as I've tried to make it, barely scratches the surface. Doing some digging on your own really draws you into your environment. Local histories abound nowadays, and their stories make fascinating campground reading. Shooting the breeze with residents in local bars and restaurants is another fun way to pick up bits of local lore.

I always carry plant, wildlife, and trail guides with me when I travel. Plant and wildlife guides truly open up the outdoors to me, helping me understand what flowers, bugs, birds, and other critters I'm seeing when I'm out there hiking, biking, and paddling the Ozarks. Without those guides my travels would be much less interesting and full of unanswered questions about what's growing by the trail, singing in the treetops, or crawling up my leg.

Trail guides are especially valuable. Reading these chapters, you'll find constant references to routes for mountain biking and hiking and rivers for canoeing and fishing. I've given brief descriptions for many, but you'll need more information to really find your way. The bibliography at the end of this book lists excellent guides that will tell you of the great trails and riverways awaiting you in the Ozarks. I also recommend obtaining national forest maps. They're great for leading you on otherwise-confusing scenic drives and finding your way on backcountry mountain bike routes. The Trails Illustrated maps of the Buffalo National River are wonderful resources for navigating that Ozarks gem. Before heading outdoors, contact the forest service, state parks, and national river offices. They have free maps of many of the trails mentioned in this guide and often sell the trail guides listed in the bibliography. Armed with some of these guides, you can explore the countryside and stay on the right path.

May your campsite always be peaceful, shady, spacious, level, and free of mosquitoes. Have fun out there!

MISSOURI STATE
PARKS

HAWN STATE PARK

Ste. Genevieve, MO

Though the campground in Hawn State Park is more developed than most of the campgrounds in this book, with many electric sites and concrete parking pads at most sites, I included it for the natural beauty of the campground and the wild atmosphere of the nearly 5,000 acres contained in the park's boundaries. Located in the flat bottom of a steep-walled hollow, the campground is nestled into a meander of Pickle Creek. Hawn State Park is named for Helen Coffer Hawn, a teacher in nearby Ste. Genevieve, who in 1952 donated the park's first 1,459 acres. Her namesake park is a wonderful place to spend a few days relaxing in nature's splendor.

As you come down the hill from the park office, the picnic area and trailhead are to your right. Downhill another 100 yards the road ends in the campground. The first loop contains nine electric sites. Just beyond that the main loop begins. The west half of the loop contains electric sites, while the east half has basic sites. Sites are spaced 50–100 feet apart. Basic sites are a little farther apart than electric sites, so they're more suitable for tenting. The best tent spots are the walk-in sites situated just beyond the east end of the loop. About 150 feet away from the parking lot, the walk-ins have more privacy, the best shade, and are near a stream that's shaded by a low sandstone bluff.

Home to one of the most popular trails in Missouri, Hawn State Park is a hiker's

CAMPGROUND RATINGS

Beauty:	★★★★★
Site privacy:	★★★
Site spaciousness:	★★★★★
Quiet:	★★★★
Security:	★★★★★
Cleanliness/upkeep:	★★★★★

Hawn State Park is home to the Whispering Pines Trail, a favorite of Missouri hikers.

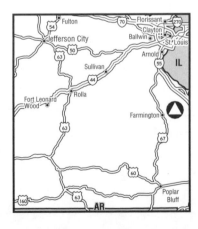

6

MISSOURI STATE PARKS

dream. Whispering Pines Trail was built in the late 1970s with the help of the Sierra Club. This 10-mile loop is everything a trail should be. You'll wander through thick stands of the shortleaf pine forests that gave the trail its name, meander along quiet streams, admire enchanting waterfalls and cascades, and be awed by spectacular vistas. One of these overlooks has two rock ledges that are the perfect place for a picnic with a view. Near its end the trail climbs to a bluff

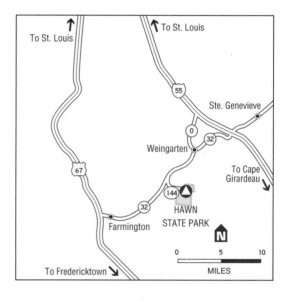

high above the campground, where you'll admire your campsite from the cliffs and anticipate enjoying a cold beverage at your picnic table after your hike.

The trail is broken into a 6-mile north loop and a 4-mile south loop. If both of those are too long for you, hike the 1-mile Pickle Creek Trail. It takes you past the most spectacular part of the park—the cascades, waterfalls, and shut-ins along Pickle Creek. It connects with the northern segment of the Whispering Pines Trail, forming a 2-mile loop. Whichever hiking option you choose, plan for wet feet if you hike in spring or after rain—all trails ford Pickle Creek at least once. It's worth getting wet, though—the deeper the streamflow, the more spectacular the cascades, and during the Ozarks summer heat and humidity, splashing through the creek is an absolute delight.

Once you've hiked all the trails at Hawn, go to the Pickle Springs Natural Area. Take MO 32 a few miles west to MO AA, and on MO AA go east 2 miles to Dorlac Road. Turn left on Dorlac and drive a half-mile to the parking area for the Trail Through Time. This spectacular 2-mile loop, a designated National Natural Landmark, is like a geological museum. If humans designed and built a landscape like this one, we'd be accused of exaggerating nature. Probably the most fascinating 2 miles in the Ozarks, the trail sports an incredible number of natural marvels crammed in a 256-acre wonderland. Best of all, it's an easy hike for novices, but so fascinating that even hardcore trampers will be enthralled.

The trail passes sandstone pillars that look like an Ozarks Bryce Canyon. You'll walk through the Slot, squeeze through a narrow gap in the stone nicknamed the Keyhole, and admire Double Arch, where two pillars support a huge sandstone ledge, forming the perfect shelter for a rainy or hot and sunny day. Owl's Den Bluff and Dome Rock overlooks give panoramic views of the surrounding forest. Mossy Falls comes to life when it rains, and another small waterfall tinkles off a small ledge near Pickle Springs itself. Just past the springs you'll come to Rockpile Canyon, where a bluff collapse created an impressive rock garden.

On all the trails in Hawn and Pickle Springs, you'll see plenty of wildflowers in spring, a lot of moss and ferns in the cool, moist areas sheltered by bluffs and rock ledges, and tremendous views from pine-studded cliffs. Bring your binoculars and bird guides when you come to Hawn State Park—many songbirds inhabit this diverse area, and you'll be lulled to sleep at night by the calls of owls and whippoorwills.

To get there: From MO 32 exit off I-55 near Ste. Genevieve, drive west 12 miles to MO 144. Turn south (left) on MO 144 and follow it 4 miles to the park. You'll pass the park office, go down a long hill, and the road will end in the campground.

KEY INFORMATION

Hawn State Park
12096 Park Drive
Ste. Genevieve, MO 63670

Operated by: Missouri DNR

Information: Park office (573) 883-3603

Open: Year-round

Individual sites: 50 total, 26 electric, 19 basic, 5 walk-in; 3 offer disabled access

Each site has: Picnic table, fire pit with grate, lantern pole

Site assignment: First come, first served, some sites reservable by phone

Registration: Park personnel or host will come by to register you and collect fee

Facilities: Water, showers, flush toilets, laundry, phone, amphitheater, picnic shelter, playground; bathhouse closed during off-season, but water and pit toilets are available

Parking: At individual site

Fee: April 1 to October 31: $7 for basic, $12 electric; November 1 to March 31: $6 basic, $10 electric; $5 fee per site when making advance reservation

Elevation: 580 feet

Restrictions:

Pets—Allowed on up to 10-foot leash

Fires—In fire pits

Alcoholic beverages—Allowed at campsites but not in public areas

Vehicles—Up to 40 feet

Other—15-day stay limit, no more than 6 persons per site

MERAMEC STATE PARK

Sullivan, MO

Meramec State Park covers 6,800 acres of wooded hills on the north side of the Meramec River. South of the river, the Meramec Conservation Area contains another 3,900 acres of Ozark countryside. Together these public lands protect 8 beautiful miles of the Meramec River. At Meramec State Park you can enjoy canoeing, hiking, mountain biking, fishing, and even exploring the Ozarks underground in one of the park's numerous caves.

Meramec is somewhat overdeveloped, as are many Ozarks state parks, but the park is so attractive that I included it anyway. It's got something for everyone. If you don't feel like cooking, head over to the dining lodge. A noncamper who wants to spend the weekend with you can rent one of the park's cabins and meet you for hikes, canoeing, or other activities in the park. At the park entrance there's an excellent visitor center with information and exhibits on the park's trails, geology, and wildlife.

Meramec's riverside campground is the east end of the developed part of the park. The first 180 sites at Meramec are in a large grassy field next to the river. This part of the campground is nice in the off-season, when it's not crowded and you appreciate direct sunshine, but it isn't good in summer. Sites are level and grassy, but are very crowded together with only scattered trees for shade.

Don't be discouraged with this huge campground—the best tent sites are ahead. Follow the camp's main road as it curves

CAMPGROUND RATINGS

Beauty:	★★★★
Site privacy:	★★
Site spaciousness:	★★★★
Quiet:	★★★★
Security:	★★★★
Cleanliness/upkeep:	★★★★★

Hiking, mountain biking, canoeing, fishing, caving— Meramec State Park and its surrounding hills have something for everybody.

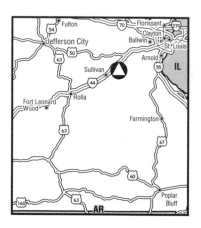

MISSOURI STATE PARKS

around and doubles back along the river past the full-hookup campsites. Just when you think you're leaving the park, you'll find two loops with great tent camping.

The first of these tent loops contains sites 181–188. The sites are level, grassy, and spacious, but some are close to the road. The second loop is where you'll find the best camping spots. Sites 189–210 are in a shady hollow next to the Meramec River, with a pretty bluff overlooking the river to the south. The openness of the sites means mini-

mal privacy, but otherwise this loop offers wonderful tent camping. Its sites are level, shady, have room for several tents, and although they seem remotely located, are the most centrally located campsites in the park. Sites 189–210 are closed during the off-season.

At the far end of the campground road, past the two best tent loops are three group camps. For a camping party with your family or friends these sites can't be beat. They're among the best group campsites I've ever seen. They're remote, heavily shaded, next to the river, and close to the showers—definitely the best campsites in the park.

The 60 miles of the Meramec River from Meramec Spring to Meramec State Park offer some of the most beautiful canoeing in Missouri. Canoe rentals are available in the park and from outfitters located up and down the Meramec. They'll set you up for single- or multi-day floats ending at your campsite in the park. You'll drift past wooded hills, farms, springs, and picturesque bluffs.

One of those bluffs towers over Green's Cave, 5 miles upstream from the campground. In my opinion, this is the prettiest place in the park. It's an easy climb to the top of the bluff to enjoy a panoramic vista of the river and fields below. Beneath you a huge cavern is hollowed out of the bluff, with a cave and spring pouring out of the bluff's back. Squeezing a few feet into the cave, you enter a large subterranean room.

You could explore farther into Green's Cave, but don't take that risk unless you're with experienced spelunkers. For a safe cave experience, go back to the park's center and tour Fisher Cave. Located next to the campground, Fisher Cave can be explored by a mile-long guided underground hike.

The park's 16 miles of hiking trails are a wonderful introduction to the Ozarks hills and forests. The Bluff View Trail showcases beautiful vistas of the river valley. The River Trail is an easy hike along the Meramec, where you're likely to spot kingfishers and herons along the river. The 10-mile Wilderness Trail has a 6-mile southern loop and a 4-mile northern loop, with overnight camps for backpackers.

Across the river in Meramec Conservation Area, there's a mountain bike trail suitable for cyclists of all skill levels. This 12-mile, two-loop trail system follows old logging roads and abandoned doubletracks through forested hills south of the river. There's also an 8-mile hiking trail in the conservation area. Both trails pass the Old Reedville School site. Marked only by a stone and a couple of logs, the site is a fascinating reminder of days gone by on the Meramec.

To get there: Drive 3 miles south of Sullivan on MO 185. Turn west into the park and follow signs to the campground.

KEY INFORMATION

Meramec State Park
2800 S. Highway 185
Sullivan, MO 63080

Operated by: Missouri DNR

Information: Park office (573) 468-6072

Open: Year-round

Individual sites: 213 sites total; 121 basic sites, 58 sites with electricity, 21 sites with full hookups, 3 group sites

Each site has: Table, fire pit with grate, lantern pole

Site assignment: First come, first served; some sites reservable by phone

Registration: Select site, leave property on site, return to entrance booth to register and pay fee

Facilities: Water, showers, flush and vault toilets, laundry, picnic area, visitor center, dining lodge, cabins, canoe rental, store, conference center

Parking: At individual site

Fee: April 1 to October 31: $7–15, $24 group; November 1 to March 31: $6–11; $5 fee for advance reservation

Elevation: 580 feet

Restrictions:

Pets—On up to a 10-foot leash; do not leash to trees

Fires—In fire pits

Alcoholic beverages—Allowed in campsites but not public areas

Vehicles—Up to 40 feet

Other—15-day stay limit, no more than 6 persons per site

ONONDAGA CAVE STATE PARK

Leasburg, MO

With more than 5,000 caves, Missouri has more subterranean beauty than any other state. And Onondaga Cave State Park has one of the most beautiful of these caverns. In 1900 a mining company bought the cave and planned to mine onyx and banded calcite. Fortunately for us, the project proved too difficult and this beautiful cave next to the Meramec River remained un-damaged.

Onondaga Cave opened to the public during the 1904 St. Louis World's Fair. It became an especially popular attraction when Lester Dill operated it in the 1950s. Before he died in 1980, Dill hoped the cave would become a state park. In 1981, through purchase by the Nature Conservancy and a subsequent transfer to the Department of Natural Resources, Onondaga became Missouri's newest natural gem.

The campground at Onondaga is especially laid-back for a state park. You can choose either an open and grassy camping loop next to the Meramec River or a more shady and secluded loop away from the stream. Sites 1–17, where all the electric sites are located, are in the riverside loop. Although only a few sites here are shady, a cooling dip in the Meramec River is only a few feet away. All sites are level and spacious but not very private. Grassy and open, they are best for campers with several tents.

Basic sites 18–73 are scattered along the floor of a long, narrow, and nicely shaded

CAMPGROUND RATINGS

Beauty:	★★★★
Site privacy:	★★★
Site spaciousness:	★★★★
Quiet:	★★★★
Security:	★★★★★
Cleanliness/upkeep:	★★★★★

Tour Onondaga Cave and admire its beautiful dripstones, flowstones, underground lake, and the spectacular Lily Pad Room.

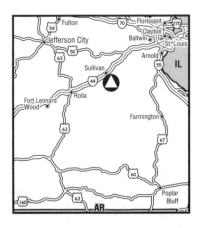

MISSOURI STATE PARKS

hollow that extends north from the Meramec River. A creek flows through the hollow and divides the two sides of this skinny campground. Few sites are private, but the loop's long and narrow configuration keeps you from having too many neighbors. Most folks set up camp near the loop entrance so they'll be closer to the river and showers. Go back to sites 36–60 at the loop's end for more privacy. Site 41 is the most secluded site at Onondaga's campground.

Absolutely do not miss the cave tour if it's open during your visit to Onondaga. Tours are offered from March to October. The cave is closed off-season to protect bat populations wintering in its caverns. If disturbed just a few times during winter, bats may use up enough energy that they might not survive until spring. Though bats get a bad rap, I love these mosquito-eating critters. When I toured the cave, one was hanging upside down just inside the entrance, giving us all a fascinating close-up look at one of these much-maligned flying mammals.

Onondaga is a beautiful cave. It's considered one of America's most spectacular caves because of the quality of its formations. On your 0.9-mile walking tour you'll see stalactites, stalagmites, flowstones, draperies, soda straws, cave coral, and underground lakes. A stream flows through Onondaga, and the Lily Pad Room, an underground lake where stalagmites and stalactites grow near circular underwater formations, is a highlight of the cave tour.

Though you'll love the cave at Onondaga, life above ground in the park is pretty good, too. Several trails traverse the park. The Blue Heron Trail is an easy half-mile hike between the campground and the visitor center, where the cave tours begin. It passes an oxbow lake in a left-behind bend of the Meramec River, where you'll often see herons fishing in the shallow waters. On this short hike you'll also see Onondaga Spring.

The other two trails begin near the shower house. The 3.25-mile Oak Ridge Trail explores the hills north of the river, showing you open glades, ridgetops, and creek bottoms. The 2.75-mile Deer Run Trail covers similar territory and has the added bonus of scenic overlooks from a bluff on the Meramec River. Deer Run also passes the locked mouth of Cathedral Cave. Sign up at the visitor center for a lantern tour of this unlighted and less developed set of caverns.

The Meramec is an excellent canoeing stream both above and below Onondaga. Huzzah and Courtois creeks pour into the Meramec a few miles upstream. I think those are even better float streams than the Meramec. They are twisty little creeks not well suited to the power boats you'll see on the deeper and wider Meramec.

You can do single- or multi-day floats on any of these three streams and land at your campsite at Onondaga, or you can push off from the park and float downstream. It's 5 miles downriver to Campbell Bridge, and 20 miles to Meramec State Park. Canoe rentals and shuttles are available from Ozark Outdoors (call (800) 888-0023) across the river from Onondaga.

To get there: From the Leasburg exit on I-44, drive 7 miles south on MO H to Onondaga Cave State Park.

KEY INFORMATION

Onondaga Cave State Park
7556 Highway H
Leasburg, MO 65535

Operated by: Missouri Department of Natural Resources

Information: Park office (573) 245-6576; Department of Natural Resources (800) 334-6946, (800) 379-2419 TDD

Open: Year-round

Individual sites: 73

Each site has: Table, fire pit with grate, lantern pole; 5 sites have electricity

Site assignment: First come, first served

Registration: Park personnel will come by to register you and collect fee

Facilities: Water, flush toilets, shower, laundry, picnic area, pavilion, amphitheater, river access, visitor center, cave, trails; bathhouse closed during off-season, but water and pit toilets are available

Parking: At individual site

Fee: April 1 to October 31: $7 basic, $12 electric; November 1 to March 31: $6 basic, $10 electric

Elevation: 640 feet

Restrictions:

Pets—Allowed on up to 10-foot leash

Fires—In fire pits

Alcoholic beverages—At site only

Vehicles—Up to 40 feet

Other—15-day stay limit; no more than 6 persons per site

SAM A. BAKER STATE PARK

Patterson, MO

Sam A. Baker State Park is named for a past governor of Missouri. Governor Baker was born in the area and pushed for the park's creation while he was in office in the mid-1920s. His namesake park, one of Missouri's oldest, is located in rugged mountains dating back to Precambrian times. When the surrounding St. Francois Mountains were formed, volcanoes dominated the landscape. Nowadays you can camp, hike, canoe, bicycle, or just hang out in the craggy forested hills where ash and lava once ruled.

All the development in this 5,164-acre state park is confined to the park's center along MO 143. The rest of Sam A. Baker State Park, including the 4,420-acre Mudlick Mountain Wild Area, remains wild and unspoiled. Even the developed central corridor is a pretty place. The dining room, cabins, and three trail shelters were built by the Civilian Conservation Corps in the 1930s, and the grounds are beautifully landscaped and maintained.

There are two campgrounds at Sam A. Baker. Campground 1 is a mile south of the park center. It contains sites 1 through 96. You'll find both basic and electric sites in Campground 1, but because these two classes of campsites are separated from each other, you can avoid camping next to an RV. Sites here aren't very far apart, but all are level, spacious, and grassy. Most are shaded for all or part of the day by a grove

CAMPGROUND RATINGS

Beauty:	★★★★★
Site privacy:	★★
Site spaciousness:	★★★★
Quiet:	★★★
Security:	★★★★★
Cleanliness/upkeep:	★★★★★

Sam A. Baker State Park is nestled in the St. Francois Mountains, one of the oldest mountain ranges in North America. While at Sam Baker, you can explore one of these ancient peaks on the Mudlick Mountain Trail.

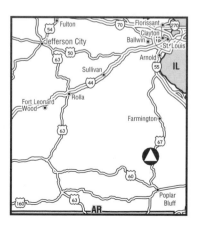

MISSOURI STATE PARKS

of mixed pines and hard-
woods. Although sites aren't
private here, Campground 1
is the least crowded and
most secluded at Sam Baker.

Sites 97–196 in Camp-
ground 2 are at the park's
center. Basic and electric sites
are mixed together throughout this camp. One spur is
basic only, but sites there are
packed tightly together and
located close to MO 143. The
best sites are at the south end
of camp, where several basic
sites are spaced well apart on
a dead-end spur. While sites
in this camp are close togeth-

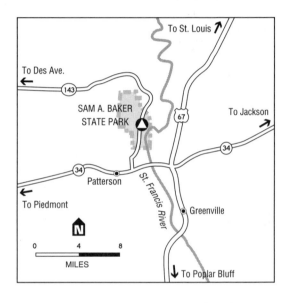

er and less private than those in Campground 1, many people prefer it because
it's close to all the park's amenities.

Visit the park's nature center to acquaint yourself with the area's flora,
fauna, and geology before you go exploring trails or streams. The center has
live snakes and turtles in terrariums, lots of skulls, rock samples, and stuffed
animals, including owls and hawks. During the park's busy season, interpretive talks and hikes are weekly features at Sam Baker.

Just north of the nature and visitor center is Sam Baker's picturesque dining
hall. Showcasing the impressive stone and log construction of 1930s-vintage
CCC architecture, it's a wonderful place to enjoy a delicious meal. Perched on
the bank of Big Creek, the dining hall sports a wonderful view of the stream
from the big windows on the east wall.

In spring Big Creek is a perfect for wading, swimming, tubing, or canoeing.
The St. Francis River meandering past the southeast part of the park near
Campground 1 is a good float year-round. The St. Francis is a raging white-
water river far upstream at Silver Mines, but by the time it reaches Sam Baker

it's a placid float all the way to Lake Wappapello. In these pretty streams, you can fish for bass, bluegill, sunfish, goggle-eye, crappie, and catfish. Canoes and tubes for exploring both streams can be rented in the park.

You can explore the park's wild area on the Mudlick Mountain National Recreation Trail, a 14-mile network of paths wandering through the landscape around Mudlick Mountain and Big and Logan creeks. A short spur leads to 1,313-foot Mudlick Mountain, where a fire tower stands sentinel in a grove of whispering pines. Highlights of this hike are three CCC-constructed stone trail shelters along the network's northeast side. These 70-year-old structures, with their mossy wood-shingle roofs, look like part of the landscape.

Even if you're not a hiker, summon the energy to hike 1 mile from the lodge to the first shelter. This shelter's setting is incredibly beautiful. It's crouched on the lip of a bluff overlooking Big Creek, with spectacular views of the stream's steep-walled valley.

Miles of mountain biking await you at Sam Baker. Just south of Campground 1 is a trailhead for the Ozark Trail. From there, the Lake Wappapello Section of the Ozark Trail travels over hills and hollows 31 miles to its southern terminus at MO 172, often skirting the shores of its namesake lake. In the south this trail connects to the Lake Wappapello Trail and the University Forest Trail, totaling more than 60 miles of scenic Ozark wandering for your two-wheeled steed.

To get there: From Patterson on MO 34, drive 4 miles north on MO 143 to Sam A. Baker State Park.

KEY INFORMATION

Sam A. Baker State Park
RFD 1, Box 114
Patterson, MO 63956

Operated by: Missouri DNR

Information: Park office (573) 856-4411

Open: Year-round

Individual sites: 196

Each site has: Table, fire pit with grate, lantern pole; 98 sites have electricity

Site assignment: First come, first served; some sites reservable

Registration: Choose site, leave property there, and go to visitor center for registration

Facilities: Water, flush and vault toilets, showers, dump station, picnic area, pavilions, store, dining room, cabins, visitor center, nature center, playgrounds, laundry, river access, canoe rental, trails; bathhouse closed in off-season, but water and pit toilets are available

Parking: At individual site

Fee: April 1 to October 31: $7 basic, $12 electric; November 1 to March 31: $6 basic, $10 electric

Elevation: 420 feet

Restrictions:

Pets—Allowed on up to 10-foot leash

Fires—In fire pits

Alcoholic beverages—Allowed at campsite but not in public areas

Vehicles—Up to 40 feet

Other—15-day stay limit

TAUM SAUK MOUNTAIN STATE PARK

Ironton, MO

With 6,500 acres in the rocky, rugged St. Francois Mountains, Taum Sauk Mountain State Park, the highest point in the state, is one of Missouri's newest and most scenic parks. This primitive, quiet campground is situated a few hundred yards from the High Point on a fairly flat part of the rounded top of the mountain. Far from any major city and at the end of a dead-end highway, Taum Sauk Mountain State Park's campground is remote and peaceful.

All 12 sites are walk-in, but since the distance from the parking areas is only 25–50 feet, it's almost like a park-in campsite. Each parking area serves two sites, which are angled away from each other to offer good spacing. These shaded and level sites are scattered along a spur off the park road, and a scout camp available for groups is located at the end of the road. Toilets and water are located at the beginning of the campground road, near the picnic area and pay station.

The park road ends a quarter mile past the campground entrance, at the parking lot for the High Point. Here you'll find more toilets and a signboard with maps and information on the park and surrounding area. A short walk on a level concrete sidewalk leads to a marker for the highest point in Missouri.

Near the marker begins the attraction that brings most visitors to this mountaintop

CAMPGROUND RATINGS

Beauty: ★★★★★
Site privacy: ★★★★
Site spaciousness: ★★★★★
Quiet: ★★★★★
Security: ★★★★
Cleanliness/upkeep: ★★★★★

At 1,772 feet, Taum Sauk Mountain State Park is the highest point in Missouri. An old fire lookout on the peak provides spectacular views of the surrounding St. Francois Mountains.

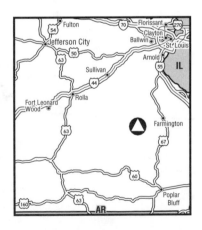

MISSOURI STATE PARKS

getaway—a spur leading to the Mina Sauk Falls Trail. This 3-mile loop descends Taum Sauk Mountain and opens up panoramic views of the surrounding countryside as you travel down to the Ozark Trail junction. One mile down the mountain you'll join the Ozark Trail at Mina Sauk Falls, a 132-foot cascade that is the highest waterfall in Missouri. The falls are truly impressive in spring, when plenty of water splashes over the rocks. I like the Mina Sauk Falls Loop best in winter, when ice sculptures form on the boulders and pools that make up the cascade.

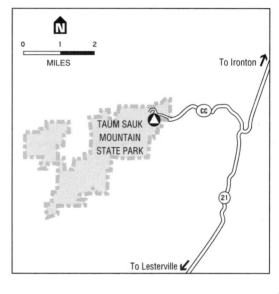

For even more spectacular scenery, continue west on the Ozark Trail. A mile west of the falls you'll pass through Devil's Tollgate. Here the trail slips through an 8-foot gap in a rock 50 feet long and 30 feet high. For even more great scenery, bring your backpack or arrange a shuttle and hike the Ozark Trail 13 miles from Taum Sauk to Johnson Shut-Ins State Park. Along the way you'll pass through open hillside glades with spectacular mountain vistas. I like hiking the long spine of Proffit Mountain, where mountain breezes cool me and ridgetop views awe me, especially in fall and winter, when the leaves are off the trees. Don't forget your hiking boots—this section of the Ozark Trail is very rugged, and sneakers won't cut it.

If you get a little worn down, no problem—the perfect anodyne awaits you at the end of the trail. You can cool those aching feet and sore muscles in the swimming holes, cascades, and fast-flowing chutes at Johnson Shut-Ins, where the Black River flows over fantastic rock formations in this other-worldly state park. After your swim, take a shower or get a cold drink and snack at the park store before heading back to the quieter, more remote Taum Sauk Mountain.

Once back at Taum Sauk State Park, grab your binoculars and climb the lookout tower to admire the terrain you just covered. Located on Department of Conservation land near the park entrance, the lookout opens up a 360-degree view of the St. Francois Mountains. The lookout shack on top is usually locked, but you can climb nearly to the top of the tower and take in the surrounding countryside. The view is especially spectacular at sunrise, when the lookout site opens, and sunset, when the area closes.

One of the more interesting landscape features visible from the lookout is the Upper Reservoir of Taum Sauk Mountain Hydroelectric Plant. What looks like a flat-topped peak is actually a man-made mountaintop lake used to generate power for the surrounding communities. If it really catches your fancy, you can see the reservoir up close via a spur off the Ozark Trail about 3 miles east of Johnson Shut-Ins.

After sunset at the tower, plan some after-dinner stargazing from the mountaintop. Far from intrusive city lights and high above the surrounding countryside, Taum Sauk offers spectacular views of night skies, especially on cold winter nights that freeze the moisture from the sky.

To get there: From Ironton, drive south 5 miles on MO 21/72 to MO CC. Turn right onto MO CC and go 4 miles to the park. The campground is 0.75 mile beyond where the pavement ends.

KEY INFORMATION

Taum Sauk Mountain State Park
c/o Johnson Shut-Ins State Park
HC Route 1, Box 126
Middlebrook, MO 63656

Operated by: Missouri Department of Natural Resources

Information: Johnson Shut-Ins State Park Office (573) 546-2450; Missouri Department of Natural Resources (800) 334-6946, (800) 379-2419 TDD

Open: Year-round; water turned off from November 1 to March 31

Individual sites: 12

Each site has: Picnic table, fire pit with grate, lantern pole

Site assignment: First come, first served

Registration: Self-pay box at campground entrance

Facilities: Water, vault toilets

Parking: Next to site, walk in 25-50 feet

Fee: April 1 to October 31: $7, November 1 to March 31: $6

Elevation: 1,700 feet

Restrictions:

Pets—Allowed on up to 10-foot leash

Fires—In fire pits

Alcoholic beverage—Allowed at campsite but not in public areas

Vehicles—No length limit

Other—15-day stay limit, no more than 6 persons per site

OZARK NATIONAL
SCENIC RIVERWAYS

BAY CREEK

Summersville, MO

Bay Creek is a bit of a secret. In conversations about the Ozark National Scenic Riverways I had only heard about Alley Spring, Big Spring, and several other expensive and crowded campgrounds along the Current and Jacks Fork rivers. It's not even listed in the park's campground information. I came here because I saw a tent symbol on the park map and thought it might be a nice spot. And it sure is!

Located where tiny Bay Creek trickles into Jacks Fork River, this backwoods hideaway doesn't have all the amenities of the huge campground at nearby Alley Spring—but it doesn't have the crowds, either. It does have swimming, wading, fishing, a huge bluff towering over the river, old two-track roads for hiking and mountain biking, and campsites so private that you might get lonely. If you do want some company or a shower, Alley is only a few miles away.

The main camp loop is on the right as you enter Bay Creek. Four of its eight sites are in a grassy meadow with shady edges, and the rest are in a shady grove between the meadow and the river. The limited privacy of the open area is their only drawback, but because Bay Creek isn't usually crowded, this isn't a problem.

For real privacy, splash through the Bay Creek ford and drive the skinny and forbidding road up the hill beyond. It climbs into a pretty bench about 20 feet above the river and follows it for almost 2 miles.

CAMPGROUND RATINGS

Beauty:	★★★★
Site privacy:	★★★★★
Site spaciousness:	★★★★★
Quiet:	★★★★★
Security:	★★★★
Cleanliness/upkeep:	★★★★

Bay Creek has four campsites so private that you might get lonesome—and it's free!

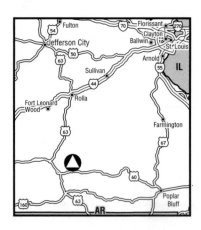

OZARK NATIONAL SCENIC RIVERWAYS

About a half mile past the main campground on your left, you'll see a great site under shade trees next to the river. It's the best site in Bay Creek. A quarter mile beyond is a new vault toilet and another very private site on the right. Another mile upriver the road ends, and there you'll find two more hideaway sites next to the Jacks Fork River. All four sites on this road are wonderfully secluded. From the last two sites it's an easy hike along gravel bars to Bee Bluff just upstream.

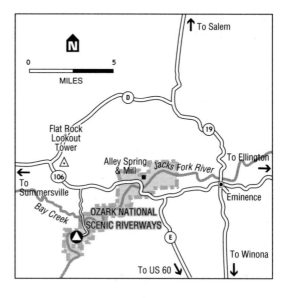

Between the last two sites a road climbs steeply to the north past the toilet, forking about 100 feet up the hill. If your car will make this road, take the left fork for a quarter mile. There you'll find an unofficial campsite—just a fire ring and a parking spot—at the base of massive Bee Bluff towering over the river. From this site you can explore a nice gravel bar in the river below the tall bluff. The right fork of this road climbs gradually to the hills north of the river. Grab your boots or bike and head up this road to explore the forests along the Ozark Scenic Riverways.

The road along the river makes Bay Creek an ideal place for tubing. Fend off summer heat by repeatedly hiking upriver and tubing the Jacks Fork back to camp. Upstream from Bay Creek is one of the most scenic and remote parts of the Jacks Fork. A 12-mile float from MO 17 down to the campground goes past Jam Up Cave, Meeting House Cave, Ebb and Flow Spring, and several impressive bluffs. On the way over to the put-in, stop at the intersection of MO 106 and MO D and climb the Flat Rock Lookout Tower for expansive vistas from 1,244 feet above sea level.

For a taste of Missouri history and folkways, drive 5 miles east to Alley Mill and Spring. You'll think you've walked into an Ozarks postcard. The bright red Alley Mill, built in 1894, rises three stories above a blue-green spring that gushes 81 million clear, cool gallons every day. The first two floors of this picturesque mill are open daily Memorial Day to Labor Day. A 0.3-mile trail goes around the spring pool and crosses the stream roaring through the old millrace. The 1.5-mile Overlook Trail climbs to the bluff 100 feet above the mill complex. Check out the spectacular view down into the spring pool and out over the valley of the spring branch, with the roar from Alley Spring's outlet drifting up from below. An interpretive display at the overlook describes life in the community that once occupied the lowlands between the spring and the river.

The old Storeys Creek School sits on the west side of the spring branch below the mill. The Alley community did have a school in the old days, but it's long gone. Storeys Creek school was moved to Alley Springs in 1971 from another location 4 miles away and is open on weekends from Memorial Day to Labor Day. It must have been a fine time at recess in those days, bolting from a hot schoolroom for a dip in the cold spring branch. Today, swimming isn't allowed in the spring branch's fragile ecosystem, but if you canoe the Jacks Fork you can see what it might have been like. Beach your canoe near the spring branch's inlet to the river and dive in. On a hot August day, you'll be gasping and grinning.

To get there: Drive 9.5 miles west from Eminence on MO 106 to a sign directing you to Bay Creek. Turn left and follow this gravel county road 2.3 miles to Bay Creek.

KEY INFORMATION

Bay Creek
Ozark National Scenic Riverways
P.O. Box 490
Van Buren, MO 63965

Operated by: National Park Service

Information: (573) 323-4236, (573) 323-4270 TDD

Open: Year-round

Individual sites: 12

Each site has: Table, fire pit with grate, trash can

Site assignment: First come, first served

Registration: No registration required

Facilities: Vault toilets, river access

Parking: At individual site

Fee: No fee

Elevation: 720 feet

Restrictions:

Pets—Allowed on up to 6-foot leash

Fires—In fire pits, rings, or pans

Alcoholic beverages—Allowed, subject to local ordinances

Vehicles—Up to 20 feet

Other—14-day stay limit; no glass containers in caves or within 50 feet of river

POWDER MILL

Owl's Bend, MO

Powder Mill is a small campground on the east bank of the Current River. Shaded by a grove of tall trees that fends off the afternoon sun, this camp is near the old Powder Mill Ferry site. A rugged bluff towers over the Current north of the MO 106 bridge, and a mile downstream the most beautiful spring in the Ozarks tumbles into the river.

The campsites are lined up along the edge of an open area bordered by deep woods on the east and riverside woods on the west. Sites are spaced about 100 feet apart, but the lack of trees between them makes for little privacy. Luckily, the small number of sites means Powder Mill doesn't feel overcrowded and noisy even when it's full. Level grassy areas around each site have plenty of room for multiple tents.

Since all sites are close to the Current, this is a fine place to ride out the heat of summer. At Powder Mill the river is wide and calm, which makes it a wonderful place to swim, wade, fish, or sunbathe. Canoeing is still fun near Powder Mill, but because of the deep waters in this stretch of the Current, power boats will often interrupt your peaceful canoeing reveries.

Powder Mill's best attractions are the nearby hiking trails. The campground is the trailhead for a 1-mile downriver hike to Blue Spring. This level footpath is an easy scenic hike, with views of the sparkling Current River on your right all the way to the spring.

CAMPGROUND RATINGS

Beauty:	★★★★
Site privacy:	★★
Site spaciousness:	★★★★
Quiet:	★★★★★
Security:	★★★★
Cleanliness/upkeep:	★★★★★

A 1-mile hike south from Powder Mill leads to spectacular Blue Spring, the deepest and most beautiful blue of the several Ozark springs sharing that name.

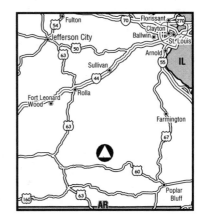

OZARK NATIONAL SCENIC RIVERWAYS

You can also reach the spring by driving 2 miles east on MO 106 to a sign directing you to Blue Spring, then 2.5 miles south on a gravel road.

However you find your way there, you'll be awed by this natural wonder. Although numerous springs in the Ozarks are called Blue Spring, this azure jewel is the bluest of them all. Viewing platforms at the spring's edge and on the low bluff above let you gaze into the pool's 250-foot depths. I like watching the small bubbles ascend from the deep on

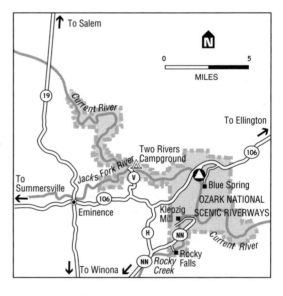

crooked paths to the pool's calm surface. Each day Blue Spring pours 90 million gallons of water into the Current River.

The Blair Creek Section of the Ozark Trail comes down from the north on the Powder Mill side of the river. At MO 106 the trail crosses the bridge, becomes the Current River Section, and continues south along the river's west side. Both these sections feature some of the prettiest hiking on the entire Ozark Trail. If you hike a mile north from the bridge, you'll have two wonderful overlooks from bluffs above Owl's Bend of the Current River. You'll see the river streaming by below, the MO 106 bridge, farms on the far side, and the Ozark Mountains marching into the distance.

Though the Current River Section is beautiful for its entire length, in its northern 10 miles you'll find two must-see sites. Historic Klepzig Mill is 7 miles from Powder Mill, and beautiful Rocky Falls is 9 miles south of Powder Mill. Both are on Rocky Creek, which flows into the Current River 5 miles downstream from Powder Mill. Don't miss Klepzig Mill and Rocky Falls.

If you're not up for hiking, you can drive to both sites. To get to Rocky Falls, drive 5 miles west on MO 106 to MO H, turn south, go 5 miles to MO NN, and then head east 5 miles to Rocky Falls. A quarter-mile drive south down a gravel road leads to the falls and a wooded picnic ground. Next to the picnic sites a wide, calm pool stretches downstream from a steel gray mass of smooth rock, over which Rocky Creek tumbles in an incredible display of cascades.

To get to Klepzig Mill, continue east on MO NN until the pavement ends. Take the left fork of two gravel roads and drive about 2 miles to the mill. You're there when you see two unpainted wooden shacks on the right side of the road. These two buildings are leftover from the early 1900s gristmill that once operated on this beautiful set of shut-ins and cascades on Rocky Creek. One of the buildings still contains some millworks, and if you work your way around the rocky shut-ins, you'll be able to pick out remains of the long-gone dam and millrace.

If you come to Klepzig Mill when it's hot, you'll enjoy sitting in the smooth rock troughs of the shut-ins and letting the cool water flow over your body. To see even more pretty scenery, hike south from the Klepzig Mill on the Ozark Trail. You'll follow Rocky Creek past pools, boulders, low bluffs, and wooded mountains on your scenic way toward Rocky Falls. It's a 1.5-mile hike to MO NN and 3 miles to Rocky Falls.

KEY INFORMATION

Powder Mill Ozark National Scenic Riverways
P.O. Box 490
Van Buren, MO 63965

Operated by: National Park Service

Information: (573) 323-4236, (573) 323-4270 TDD

Open: Year-round

Individual sites: 8

Each site has: Table, fire pit with grate, lantern pole

Site assignment: First come, first served

Registration: Self-pay at campground entrance

Facilities: Water, vault toilets, river access, trails; water turned off during winter

Parking: At individual site

Fee: $12

Elevation: 560 feet

Restrictions:

Pets—Allowed on up to 6-foot leash

Fires—In fire pits

Alcoholic beverages—Allowed, subject to local ordinances

Vehicles—Up to 40 feet

Other—14-day stay limit; no glass containers in caves or within 50 feet of river

To get there: From Eminence, drive 12 miles east on MO 106. The campground entrance is on the right just east of the Current River Bridge.

PULLTITE

Eminence, MO

I f you like to camp near streams, Pulltite is the place for you. This long, narrow campground stretches along a bend of the Current River. Across the river are historic Pulltite Cabin and Spring, where gristmills operated from the mid-1800s until 1911. Powered by the spring's daily 20–30 million gallon outflow, this mill deep in the river valley indirectly gave the area its unique name. It was a "tight pull" for mules and horses pulling wagonloads of ground meal from the mill to the hillsides above the village of Pulltite.

This campground is a nice one, but sites are a little crowded and the openness of the area limits privacy. These disadvantages are offset by the campground's layout. Pulltite's long and narrow configuration keeps it from feeling crowded when it's full. Most sites are level spaces in nice grassy areas. If you like to be near the action, settle into sites 1–13. They are in a small, well-shaded loop near the river access and campground entrance. A small store and canoe rental service operates next to these sites.

Sites 14–42 are located on both sides of the gravel road leading to the back of the campground. Though they're close to the road, many are excellent sites with shade and proximity to the river. Those on the south side back up to woods, while the sites on the north are next to the river across from a low bluff. Sites 44–55 are in another

CAMPGROUND RATINGS

Beauty:	★★★★
Site privacy:	★★
Site spaciousness:	★★★
Quiet:	★★★
Security:	★★★★
Cleanliness/upkeep:	★★★★★

All of Pulltite's 55 campsites are only a few steps from the cool, spring-fed Current River.

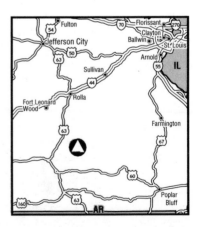

OZARK NATIONAL SCENIC RIVERWAYS

small loop near the end of the campground. Like sites 1–13, they're packed fairly close together. Site 55 at the back of the loop offers most privacy.

The group sites are the best camping spots at Pulltite. Group camp 3, at the very end of the campground road, is a remote site right on the river's edge. Whether you camp in the group or single sites, you'll be glad to know that the park service plans to install showers at Pulltite in the near future. For now, you're limited to

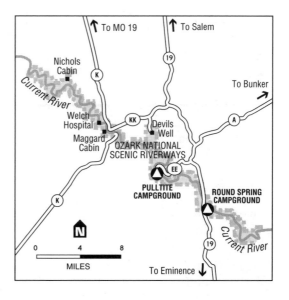

swimming in the river or driving south to Round Spring Campground.

Group camp 3 is the trailhead for the 1.5-mile Pulltite Trail. It's a relatively easy hike following the banks of the Current for a third of its length before climbing into the hills east of the river. On the northeast side of the loop you'll see an intermittent spring trickling from a small box canyon, and just south of the spring is a cave. In summer the cave entrance is a cool place, and on cold winter days it breathes warm moist air on your face.

During your stay at Pulltite be sure to check out Pulltite Spring and Cabin. Since it's across the Current from camp, you'll have to wade or canoe to check out this historic site. Splashing through the cool, spring-fed river is a delight on hot and humid summer days.

Great canoeing awaits you at Pulltite. You can paddle the scenic upper Current River on floats of varying lengths and end up here. Pulltite is 24 miles from Baptist, 17 miles from Cedargrove, and 10 miles from Akers. If the river's flowing strongly you could paddle the whole distance from Baptist but wouldn't have time to relax or explore along the way. Current River is best done in sections or as a two-day float.

Take your time on the river, because there are several things you shouldn't miss. One of these is fishing—from Baptist to Akers the cool spring-fed Current contains trout. From Baptist to Cedargrove it's a trophy trout management area.

About 5 miles downriver from Baptist on your left you'll see Parker Hollow, where a small creek pours into the Current. A short walk up the hollow goes to the historic Nichols Cabin, an abandoned Ozarks farmstead restored in the 1980s.

Five river miles below Cedargrove Access is Welch Spring and Hospital, another haunting ruin on the Current. Built over a cave next to a 75 million gallon-per-day spring, the remains of this early-twentieth-century hospital are fascinating to explore. An Illinois doctor built the hospital with the belief that spring waters and the cool, clean air from the cave had medicinal healing qualities.

A half mile downriver from Welch Spring is Welch Landing. Directly across the river from the landing is the Howell-Maggard Cabin Stabilization Project, another abandoned homesite like Nichols Cabin. Restoration of this farmstead began in 2000. Cave Spring is 5 miles below Akers. The pool at the back of the cave is more than 100 feet deep. This spring draws its water from nearby Devils Well, another site you shouldn't miss while camping in the Ozark Riverways.

To get there: From Salem drive 25 miles south on MO 19 to MO EE. Turn west on MO EE and follow it 4 miles to Pulltite.

KEY INFORMATION

Pulltite
Ozark National Scenic Riverways
P.O. Box 490
Van Buren, MO 63965

Operated by: National Park Service

Information: (573) 323-4236, (573) 323-4270 TDD

Open: Year-round

Individual sites: 55 single sites, 3 group sites

Each site has: Table, fire pit with grate, lantern pole

Site assignment: First come, first served

Registration: Self-pay at campground entrance

Facilities: Water, vault toilets, river access, trail, camp store and canoe rental during summer months; water turned off during winter

Parking: At individual site

Fee: $12

Elevation: 740 feet

Restrictions:

Pets—Allowed on up to 6-foot leash

Fires—In fire pits, rings, or pans

Alcoholic beverages—Allowed, subject to local ordinances

Vehicles—No specified limit, but most sites not suitable for vehicles larger than 20 feet

Other—14-day stay limit; no glass containers in caves or within 50 feet of river

ROUND SPRING

Eminence, MO

Long before there was an Ozark National Scenic Riverways, Missourians realized Round Spring was a treasure. In 1924 this scenic jewel near the banks of the Current River became one of Missouri's first state parks. Named for the shape of the pool from which it flows, Round Spring wells gently from the earth at a rate of 26 million gallons daily, flows through a fissure in the wall surrounding its pool, and meanders into the Current River.

The main campground at Round Spring is beautiful. For a well-developed campground it's a surprisingly laid-back place. Sites are a little close together, but landscaping and thick woods make things feel fairly private. It's built into a hillside above the river, with many sites terraced above or below the camp road, thus creating a more isolated atmosphere. The paved road eliminates dust and the annoying crunch of tires on gravel.

Sites on the main loop road are more private and well shaded. Sites 51–60 are on the road that bisects the loop; they are open and poorly shaded. Sites 43–48 are walk-in camping spots. Site 25, with a nice view of the Current River, is my favorite spot at Round Spring.

Across Spring Creek from the main campground are the cluster campsites. They are level but offer little shade or privacy. The exceptionally nice group campsites are across the river and the highway, north of the

CAMPGROUND RATINGS

Beauty:	★★★★
Site privacy:	★★★★
Site spaciousness:	★★★
Quiet:	★★★★
Security:	★★★★
Cleanliness/upkeep:	★★★★★

Sixty years before it became part of the Ozark National Scenic Riverways, Round Spring was one of Missouri's first state parks.

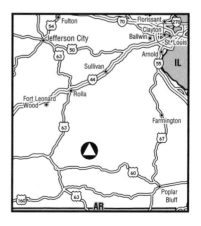

31

OZARK NATIONAL SCENIC RIVERWAYS

main recreation area and next to the store and canoe rental service. Located right on the river's edge, Round Spring's group camps are wonderful sites.

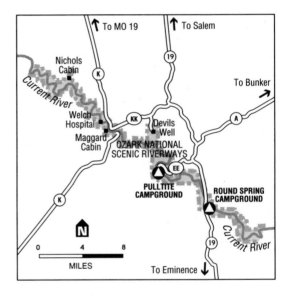

The campgrounds and attractions at Round Spring are connected by a trail paralleling MO 19. This path crosses the Current River and Spring Creek on pedestrian bridges arching high above the streams. The trail is a handy thing—you can hike it from the main campground to the group camps, then jump into the Current for a half-mile tubing run back to camp.

Although the Ozarks are full of caves, many folks are afraid to venture alone into one. That's not a problem here—just west of the campground is Round Spring Cave, where you can take a tour to admire the underground beauty of the Ozarks. Guided forays into the cave are offered daily June through August.

The Current has plenty of bass and sunfish, but for a real angling challenge head to the upper river. The cold spring waters there support a state-managed trout fishery. Much of the river is inaccessible by road, so you'll have more opportunities if you canoe to your fishing spots. From Baptist Access to Cedargrove the river is a trophy trout management area, where only artificial baits can be used. From Cedargrove to Akers the Current is a regular trout management area. Study and follow all Missouri fishing rules and regulations.

While canoeing the Current, you'll pass Cave Spring about 5 miles downstream from Akers. It draws its water from Devils Well, a must-see while camping in the Ozark Riverways. You can reach the well by driving north from Round Spring on MO 19 to MO KK, then turning west on KK to a gravel road with a sign directing you 1.5 miles to Devils Well.

Once at Devils Well, you'll see a staircase descending into the bowels of the earth. Sinkholes are all over the Ozarks, but rarely can you enter one. Here you'll go underground and peer into a deep pool 100 feet below. A light switch lets you flood the chamber with light to admire the sight and sound of hundreds of water droplets showering from the chamber's ceiling into the pool below.

A must-see historical site near Devils Well is Welch Hospital, built over a cave's mouth next to the 75 million-gallon-per-day flow of Welch Spring. Believing that the moist cave air and clear spring water had medicinal properties, Dr. C. H. Diehl built this hospital in the early 1900s. Two miles north of Akers on MO K and a half mile west on a gravel road is Welch Landing. From there it's a pretty half-mile hike upstream to this abandoned hospital. The spring is beautiful, gurgling from the base of a 25-foot bluff and flowing 200 feet to the river. A ledge on the bluff makes a perfect overlook of the hospital ruin and the spring's cascade into the Current River.

Across the river from Welch Landing is the Howell-Maggard Cabin Stabilization Project. The cabin is thought to have been built in the 1850s, and the land around it farmed by the Howell family until the 1930s. Owned by Earl Maggard until the park service bought it in 1969, the cabin began undergoing restoration in 2000. Walk around this old homesite and your thoughts will drift back to old times in the Ozarks.

To get there: From Salem, drive 30 miles south on MO 19. From Eminence, drive 13 miles north on MO 19.

KEY INFORMATION

Round Spring Ozark National Scenic Riverways
P.O. Box 490
Van Buren, MO 63965

Operated by: National Park Service

Information: (573) 323-4236, (573) 323-4270 TDD

Open: Year-round

Individual sites: 54 single sites, 6 walk-in sites, 9 cluster sites, 3 group sites

Each site has: Table, fire pit with grate, lantern pole

Site assignment: First come, first served; reservations required for group sites

Registration: Self-pay at campground entrance

Facilities: Water, flush and vault toilets, picnic area, pavilion, river access, trails; showers, canoe rental, store, dump station, and laundry facilities in summer months

Parking: At individual site

Fee: $12 single site; cluster sites $20 for up to 10 campers, $2 each additional person, maximum 20 people

Elevation: 700 feet

Restrictions:

Pets—On up to 6-foot leash

Fires—In fire pits

Alcoholic beverages—Allowed, subject to local ordinances

Vehicles—Up to 30 feet

Other—14-day stay limit; no glass containers in caves or within 50 feet of river

MARK TWAIN NATIONAL FOREST

BERRYMAN TRAIL

Potosi, MO

The Berryman Trail Campgrounds are two separate camps located 7 miles apart on the Berryman Trail, a 24-mile loop popular with hikers, mountain bikers, and equestrians. Both these beautiful getaways are perfect jumping-off points for exploring the Berryman Trail.

My favorite is the Brazil Creek Camp. Its drawback is its popularity with equestrians. On some weekends the camp is jammed with stock trailers and pickups. If you like to ride, it's the place to be. When there are no big rides, it's a peaceful setting. Tall stately pines, sighing gently in the breeze, shelter the open camping area next to Brazil Creek. All sites are grassy, shaded, and have room for several tents. The creek is a nice place for a cooling wade on the hot days. I like it here in winter, too, when it's quiet and tranquil.

When horse trailers make Brazil Creek too crowded, I opt for Berryman Camp, located at the southern end of the trail. It has no water source, so it's usually free of equestrians. It's rarely full, and campsites are scattered in the woods. Trees separate the sites, so privacy is better than at Brazil Creek. An open picnic area at Berryman offers great stargazing, and there's a small picnic pavilion for escaping rainy weather. Berryman is the old campsite of CCC Company 3733. The picnic pavilion is dedicated to the men who worked here in the 1930s.

These camps are great places to hang out and enjoy the outdoors, but their big attrac-

CAMPGROUND RATINGS

Beauty: ★★★
Site privacy: ★★★
Site spaciousness: ★★★★
Quiet: ★★★★★
Security: ★★★★
Cleanliness/upkeep: ★★★★

The Berryman Trail Campgrounds are located on the Berryman Trail, the most popular backcountry mountain biking ride in Missouri.

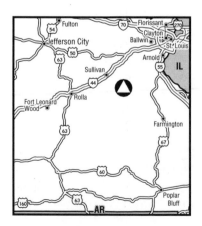

MARK TWAIN NATIONAL FOREST

tion is the Berryman Trail. A longtime favorite with hikers, it has now become the most popular backcountry mountain biking trail in the state. Some short trails near the urban areas get more use, but the Berryman is known statewide as the trail to pedal in the Show Me State.

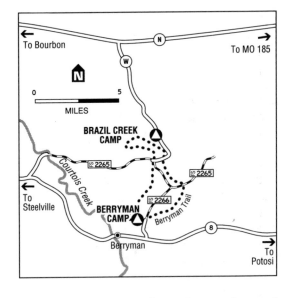

With many climbs, rock-strewn technical sections, and a satisfying length, the Berryman is ideal for experienced riders. It's a tough ride for novices, but beginners with a good attitude will like the Berryman very much. Since numerous road crossings make good places to bail out, the trail is good for beginners to try their first backcountry single-track challenge.

Almost all of the Berryman Trail is single-track. Some stretches are rough and rocky, but few will require portaging your bike. Because the trail alternates between ridgetops and creek bottoms, the scenery includes both pleasant meandering streams and beautiful views from the tops of the climbs. Many stretches of the trail are carved out of the shoulders of ridges, skirting deep, quiet hollows in the forest. Your ride will swoop around the tops of hollows, plunge to valley floors, and pass two springs.

The Berryman is a great hike, too. You can do it in one day, but only if you work like a dog. Most hikers doing the entire trail make it a two-day backpack trip. My favorite day hike uses the northern part of the trail, starting from Brazil Creek. Hike from the camp 1.5 miles up MO W to where it ends at FS 2265. About 100 feet past there, pick up the trail where it crosses FS 2265, turn right, and hike back to camp. On the way you'll pass by Harmon Spring, through quiet hillside pine groves, and end the 8-mile-loop hike by descending steeply back to Brazil Creek on a nice set of switchbacks.

Just before the descent to Brazil Creek, the gravel on the trail is very flinty. On a night hike one winter evening I noticed from the corner of my eye faint glints of light. Looking down, I noticed that every scuff of my boot on the rocky treadway was striking tiny sparks. Take a night hike on the Berryman and kick up your own light show—the woods are a completely different kind of beautiful under dark, starry skies!

A fascinating trail highlight is Edward Beecher Spring. Actually an artesian well, Beecher is in a pretty meadow. An iron casing with a pipe extending from the side of the well constantly disgorges cool, clear water into a small trough. It's a nice place for lunch on your hiking or biking excursion. Beecher is about 6 miles north from Berryman Camp and 2 miles south of the FS 2265 crossing.

Several good canoeing streams are close by, too. Huzzah Creek, 9 miles west of Berryman Camp on MO 8, and Courtois Creek, about 8 miles west of Brazil Creek on FS 2265, are laid-back little creeks just big enough for canoes.

To get there: To reach Berryman Camp from Potosi, head west on MO 8 for 17 miles, then go 1 mile north on FS 2266. Brazil Creek Camp is 17 miles south of Sullivan on MO 185, then 8 miles west on MO N, then 9 miles south on MO W. To drive from Berryman Camp to Brazil Creek Camp, go 3 miles northeast on FS 2266, 3 miles northwest on FS 2265, then 1 mile northeast on MO W.

KEY INFORMATION

Berryman Trail Campgrounds
Mark Twain National Forest
P.O. Box 188
Potosi, MO 63664

Operated by: U.S. Forest Service

Information: (573) 438-5427

Open: Year-round

Individual sites: 8 at Berryman Camp, 8 at Brazil Creek Camp

Each site has: Table, lantern pole, fire pit with grate

Site assignment: First come, first served

Registration: No registration required

Facilities: Vault toilets at both campgrounds, no water; Berryman Camp has picnic area with pavilion

Parking: At individual site

Fee: $5 at Berryman Camp; donations accepted at Brazil Creek Camp

Elevation: Berryman Camp 1,000 feet, Brazil Creek 900 feet

Restrictions:

Pets—Allowed on leash

Fires—In fire pit

Alcoholic beverages—Allowed, subject to local ordinances

Vehicles—Up to 25 feet

Other—14-day stay limit

BIG BAY

Shell Knob, MO

Big Bay Recreation Area sits on a small peninsula in beautiful Table Rock Lake. Table Rock is a sparkling 53,000-acre reservoir with snakelike arms pushing deep into the surrounding hills and hollows. Big Bay is named for Big Creek, the stream submerged beneath the cove next to the campground. Table Rock's waters, extraordinarily clean for such a large inland lake, are so clear that scuba divers come here to explore the lake's depths.

Big Bay is a nice escape from the touristy commercial sites scattered along the shores of Table Rock. RV campers usually choose one of the many lakeside RV parks with full hookups. Big Bay enjoys the happy combination of rustic and peaceful national forest campsites only a few miles from the enjoyable amenities of the commercial resorts on the lake.

All sites at Big Bay are nicely shaded by the thick forest covering the hills around the lake. In spite of the trees, most sites have nice views of Table Rock Lake. The road into Big Bay forks at the campground entrance. Each of these forks is a dead-end road with campsites scattered on both sides.

The right fork contains sites 1–20. All its campsites are shady, level, and separated by 100 feet of brush and trees. Except for sites 16–18, which are crowded together near the rest rooms, all are very private. The landscape slopes from the sites to the water's edge, giving many sites views of

CAMPGROUND RATINGS

Beauty:	★★★★
Site privacy:	★★★★★
Site spaciousness:	★★★★
Quiet:	★★★★
Security:	★★★★
Cleanliness/upkeep:	★★★★★

Big Bay is a quiet enclave on the shores of beautiful Table Rock Lake.

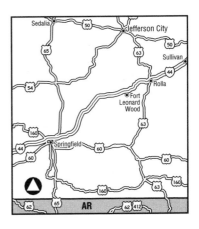

MARK TWAIN NATIONAL FOREST

the lake through the trees. Sites 1–3 at the end of the road are the most spacious, roomy, and scenic camping spots on this fork.

Sites 20–35 on the left fork are better yet. They are farther apart and offer even better views of Table Rock Lake. Shaded by thick pines and hardwoods, they have level and roomy spots for tents. This arm of camp is cut into a hillside with campsites terraced above and below the road, which creates a cozy and private atmosphere. The best spot at Big Bay is site 35 at the end of the fork. This shady and secluded camping spot is set back into the woods above the road. Sites 36 and 37 are the only really poor sites in Big Bay. They're cramped sites located near the fork, where all the campground traffic passes them.

No matter where you camp in this pretty recreation area, you'll never be far from one of the numerous water faucets dispersed throughout the campground. At the day-use area you'll find scenic picnic sites, where tables scattered under shade trees overlook the lake next to the boat ramp. Just west of the boat ramp a gravel beach slopes into the lake. It's a good swimming spot, but since it drops off quickly it's not a great place for kids. A better swimming beach is at Campbell Point, an Army Corps of Engineers recreation site located 1 mile farther down MO YY.

Anglers will love the fishing in Table Rock Lake. The lake is loaded with various game fishes, including several varieties of bass, crappie, walleye, and catfish. You'll need a boat to take best advantage of the fishery at Table Rock. Big Bay is fun to explore via canoe, but a motorboat is best for exploring the hundreds of miles of shoreline on the lake.

There are no trails in the campground, but 10 miles north of Big Bay on MO 39 and MO 76 is the Big Piney Wilderness. The Big Piney's 8,400 acres cover the entire watershed of Big Piney Creek—a rocky Ozark stream pouring into the James River Arm of Table Rock Lake at the east end of the wilderness area.

This lakeshore wildland is laced with 13 miles of trails. The best hike is the 6-mile loop connecting the northern trailhead at the Piney Lookout Tower with the southern Siloam Springs trailhead. Piney Creek cuts across the center of this loop, and a trail along the creek provides two 3-mile loop options. On the Big Piney trails you'll follow ridges, descend into hollows, splash through streams, and pass several springs.

Big Bay isn't far from Roaring River State Park. It's worth the 20-mile drive to check out Roaring River Spring. It gushes 20 million gallons daily, feeding enough cool water into the river to support a trout population that's just waiting for your fly rod. For the hiker, numerous trails ranging in length from 0.7 to 3.5 miles lace the park. The Devil's Kitchen Interpretive Trail, named for a fascinating rock-walled hideout used by Civil War guerillas, is a great hike. It showcases the hideout and other geologic wonders, including a shelter cave and a spring cave.

KEY INFORMATION

Big Bay Recreation Area
Mark Twain National Forest
P.O. Box 188
Business Route 5 S.
Ava, MO 65608

Operated by: U.S. Forest Service

Information: (417) 683-4428

Open: May 1–October 15

Individual sites: 37

Each site has: Table, fire pit with grate, lantern pole

Site assignment: First come, first served

Registration: Self-pay at campground entrance

Facilities: Water, flush toilets, lake access

Parking: At individual site

Fee: $10 per site

Elevation: 950 feet

Restrictions:

Pets—Allowed on leash

Fires—In fire pits

Alcoholic beverages—Allowed, subject to local ordinances

Vehicles—Up to 40 feet

Other—14-day stay limit

To get there: From MO 39 in Shell Knob, drive 2.5 miles east on MO YY. Turn left on a paved road with a sign directing you to Big Bay and follow it a half mile to the campground.

COUNCIL BLUFFS

Belgrade, MO

Council Bluffs Recreation Area is built around the 440-acre Council Bluffs Lake on the Big River. Opened in 1985, Wild Boar Ridge Campground is a group of campsites strung along the spine of a forested Ozark ridge above the lake. Stretching over a mile-long ridge instead of being crammed into the tight cluster we've come to expect in public campgrounds, sites in Wild Boar Campground are comfortably far apart. All have ample level space for tents. Though many sites are large enough for RVs, lack of hookups keeps most RVs away. When a behemoth does show up, good spacing between sites and thick woods between camps keep things private and peaceful.

The most secluded sites are the nine walk-in sites. They have all the amenities of the vehicle sites, but are tucked back in the woods off the main loop and spaced at least 100 feet apart. If you want solitude, these sites are worth hauling your stuff a few yards. The most secluded vehicle camps are sites 25 through 35 at the far end of the road. My favorite is site 32 at the very end of the road.

No matter where you camp, you're never far from the water faucets and toilets scattered throughout this well-designed campground. I especially like the cooking shelters at all sites. They're little but have shelves big enough to store your cooking gear, covered with just enough roof to protect you and your grub from downpours while you whip up your outdoor cuisine. When it's clear,

CAMPGROUND RATINGS

Beauty:	★★★★
Site privacy:	★★★★★
Site spaciousness:	★★★★
Quiet:	★★★★
Security:	★★★★★
Cleanliness/upkeep:	★★★★★

The trail around Council Bluffs Lake connects to the Ozark Trail, opening up miles and miles of back-country hiking and biking.

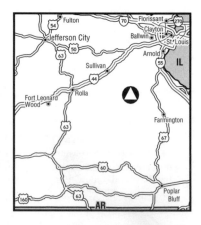

MARK TWAIN NATIONAL FOREST

you won't need any shelter from the hot sun—all sites are heavily shaded.

If you get bored at Council Bluffs, you need help. Maybe I need help, because I think even being bored here is fun! Take a book out to the sandy beach and relax on the sand. Drag your lawn chair to one of the small promontories on the lake's edge and listen to the waves lapping at the shore. Watch the trees around the campsite sway in the ridge-top breezes.

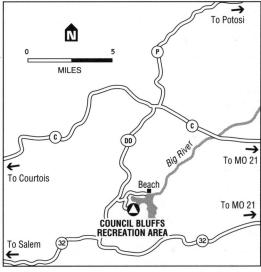

Feeling a little more active? Take a swim at Chapel Hill Beach and Picnic Area. The sandy beach is perfect for bare feet, and the lake is clear and sparkling blue. You can walk the 3 miles from Wild Boar Campground to the beach on the Council Bluffs Trail. Those wanting a longer excursion can hike all the way around the lake on this 12.5-mile path. In many places it follows the shoreline, with constant scenic views of blue water and green hillsides. Snags stretching up out of the water in the coves serve as roosts for woodpeckers, kingfishers, herons, and the occasional hawk or osprey. The trail doesn't have a lot of ups and downs, so it's not too difficult to hike.

The Council Bluffs Trail is open to mountain bikes, too. It's become a favorite ride for cyclists out of St. Louis. While it is a moderate trail for hiking, it's a tough bike ride. Though there isn't a lot of climbing, the rocky and rugged surface requires good bike-handling skills and will beat you up a little. If you're a novice, just ride the part between the campground and the beach—it's not too hard and is the prettiest stretch. Two spur trails connect the campground to the trail. One spur leaves the camp road next to the horseshoe pits, and the other drops off the ridge at the end of the campground road.

The Ozark Trail passes within a half mile of Council Bluffs Lake. A half-mile spur along Telleck Branch connects it to the Council Bluffs Trail, opening up miles and miles of Ozarks hiking and biking. For another good novice ride, follow the Council Bluffs Trail from the campground to the connector trail, then follow it west to the Ozark Trail. Turn north on the Ozark Trail and follow it north to MO DD, where you can turn right and ride the highway and Council Bluffs Recreation Area roads back to the campground to complete a 6-mile loop.

If you tire of the trails in the Council Bluffs, check out the nearby Bell Mountain Wilderness Area, where a 5-mile one-way hike will take you to Missouri's second-highest point. Use the Ottery Creek Trailhead for the Ozark Trail on MO A 6 miles south of MO 32. From Ottery Creek, the first mile of the Ozark Trail switchbacks steeply uphill, opening up vistas that make the trip worthwhile all by themselves. Just over a mile up the mountainside the trail forks, and the Ozark Trail bears right. Take the left fork and continue uphill, climbing gradually to the top of Bell Mountain, 1,702 feet above sea level. It's a tough climb, but along the way you'll enjoy long-distance vistas from open glades on an impressive boulder-strewn plateau. Once off the Ozark Trail, the route isn't marked, so it's a good idea to bring a map or Missouri hiking guide.

To get there: From Potosi, drive south on MO P to MO C. Go west on MO C a quarter mile to MO DD. On MO DD go south 7 miles to Council Bluffs Recreation Area and follow the signs 1.8 miles to Wild Boar Ridge Campground.

KEY INFORMATION

Council Bluffs Recreation Area
Mark Twain National Forest
P.O. Box 188
Potosi, MO 63664

Operated by: U.S. Forest Service

Information: (573) 438-5427

Open: May 1–October 15

Individual sites: 39 single sites, 7 double, 9 walk-in, 4 group

Each site has: Picnic table, fire pit with grate, lantern pole, cooking shelter

Site assignment: First come, first served; reservations available at (877) 444-6777 or ReserveUSA.com

Registration: Pay campground host at site 1

Facilities: Water, vault toilets, picnic area, horseshoe pits, playing field, pavilion, swimming beach, boat ramp

Parking: At site; separate parking lots for walk-in sites

Fee: $8 single, $16 double, $25 group, $8.65 reservation fee (nonrefundable); $2 per vehicle at boat ramp, trailhead, and beach parking areas

Elevation: 1,300 feet

Restrictions:

Pets—Allowed on leash; no pets on beach

Fires—In fire pits

Alcoholic beverages—Allowed, subject to local ordinances

Vehicles—Up to 40 feet

Other—14-day stay limit; no glass containers or coolers on beach

DEER LEAP AND FLOAT CAMP RECREATION AREAS

Doniphan, MO

If lazing in the shade next to a beautiful river is your idea of a good time, you'll like Deer Leap and Float Camp. Located next to the wide, deep reaches of the lower Current River, these campsites are comfortable streamside hideaways. Deer Leap and Float Camp are two separate recreation areas in the Mark Twain National Forest. Since they're only a half mile apart, I decided to lump them together as a single campground.

Float Camp is the best loop for families. Its 16 sites are in an open area shaded with tall hardwoods. At each site there's plenty of room for several tents. While the open area limits privacy, good spacing between sites keeps you from feeling crowded. Several sites with table shelters are great camping spots on rainy days. The best spot in Float Camp is site 8. Located at the end of the campground road's turn-around loop and close to the river, it's the loop's most private camp.

This flat-bottomed hollow next to the Current River is a wonderful enclave, with room to toss a Frisbee or play catch. Horseshoe pits are located behind site 16. The river is only a few steps away, and a gently sloping gravel beach makes this a great swimming hole. A shady path crosses a bridge between the campground and the beach, passing through a small alcove in the woods with benches overlooking the river. The alcove is a perfect spot to admire

CAMPGROUND RATINGS

Beauty:	★★★★
Site privacy:	★★★★
Site spaciousness:	★★★★★
Quiet:	★★★★
Security:	★★★★
Cleanliness/upkeep:	★★★★★

Float Camp and Deer Leap are wonderful places for floating, fishing, or swimming in the lower reaches of the beautiful Current River.

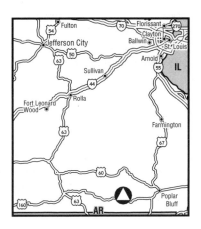

MARK TWAIN NATIONAL FOREST

the river and watch the kids as they splash in the stream.

A nice riverside path leads from camp to the picnic area. There you'll find a shelter, picnic sites, more swimming, changing rooms, and a sand volleyball court. The water's deeper near the picnic area, with hidden drop-offs, so be careful.

Float Camp's only drawback is its lack of drinking water. But you can tank up at Deer Leap Campground, where taps are open May through October. Deer Leap, with only 13 sites, is quieter and more private than Float Camp. Its sites are a little farther apart and are separated by belts of woods. Deer Leap doesn't have nice swimming areas like Float camp, and it lacks amenities such as picnic sites, pavilions, and volleyball courts. Consequently, while both these cool and shady riverside camps may be full on hot summer weekends, Deer Leap is likely to be the more peaceful of the two. Site 9, at the end of the campground road right at the river's edge, is my favorite site at Deer Leap.

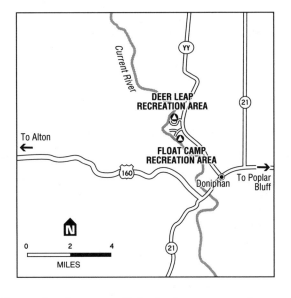

The blue waters of the Current make these camping loops wonderful summer hangouts. Tubing is a great way to enjoy the campgrounds. At Float Camp, use the trail between the picnic area and campground for short runs without a shuttle. You can do the same at Deer Leap, bobbing along the river from the head of the campground to the river access for a half-mile run, then walking the road back to camp. Using a shuttle driver lets you float the Current from site 9 at Deer Leap to the camping loop at Float Camp on a 1-mile tubing run.

While this part of the Current River is tamer than its upper reaches in the Ozark National Scenic Riverways, it still offers great canoeing. Fewer gravel bars and obstructions make it a better float for families with small children. It's an easy 5-mile paddle to Doniphan, where you can have an ice-cream cone before heading back to camp. Local outfitters can shuttle you upriver for longer trips back to your campsite at Float Camp and Deer Leap. The wider and deeper reaches of the lower Current offer excellent fishing, too. Bring along your fishing gear and go after the bass, sunfish, buffalo, and catfish that hide in the river below your canoe.

Two short trails at Float Camp explore the forest around the campground. The half-mile Woodchuck Trail follows the river between the camp and the day-use area, then climbs the hills above to overlook the Current. The 1.5-mile White Oak Trail explores the hills east of the campground. Near the trailhead at the picnic area, the White Oak Trail passes Malden Spring. Though not as impressive as its brothers Alley, Greer, and Big Springs, Malden is still a pretty little trickler pouring 8,000 gallons daily into the Current River.

If you're not into water sports, try volleyball or horseshoes. A horseshoe pit and a volleyball court are available at KC's on the Current, a store and canoe outfitter on MO YY at the entrance to Float Camp. KC's manages the campgrounds and can outfit you for floating, tubing, or fishing while you're enjoying the Ozarks at Deer Leap and Float Camp Recreation Areas.

To get there: Take MO YY 4.5 miles north of Doniphan. Deer Leap's entrance is a half mile past Float Camp. Both are on the west side of the highway.

KEY INFORMATION

Deer Leap and Float Camp Recreation Areas
Mark Twain National Forest
1104 Walnut
Doniphan, MO 63935

Operated by: U.S. Forest Service

Information: (573) 996-2153

Open: Year-round

Individual sites: 29

Each site has: Table, fire pit with grate, lantern pole; some sites in Float Camp have table shelters

Site assignment: First come, first served

Registration: Self-pay at loop entrances

Facilities: Vault toilets, river access at both campgrounds; water available only at Deer Leap; Float Camp has picnic area, pavilion, playground, volleyball nets, horseshoe pits, trails; water turned off November through April

Parking: At individual site

Fee: $8 per site; $2 per vehicle in day-use areas

Elevation: 350 feet

Restrictions:

Pets—Allowed on leash

Fires—In fire pits

Alcoholic beverages—Allowed, subject to local ordinances

Vehicles—Up to 24 feet

Other—14-day stay limit; no glass containers at swimming areas

GREER CROSSING

Winona, MO

Greer Crossing Recreation Area is smack in the middle of one of my favorite landscapes in Missouri—the Eleven Point Wild and Scenic River country. Greer Crossing, with upper access for canoeing the most beautiful section of the Eleven Point, is the perfect base for exploring the hills and hollows near the river. Located a few hundred feet from the river, Greer's sites are level, well spaced, and shady. Most of these spacious grassy sites have room for two or more tents. Walls of trees and brush separate you from the neighbors. No sites are directly on the Eleven Point, but it's only a short walk to a dip at the nearby picnic area and river access.

The water is refreshing, but you'll be out in a hurry—most of the Eleven Point's flow gushes from the 30 springs that feed it, keeping the river cold on the hottest summer day. Put on your waders and come back, though, because the cool water provides a rare pleasure in the Midwest—a wild trout population just waiting for you to try your hand at fly-fishing.

If you don't have waders, go after those trout in a canoe. Whether you are fishing or just drifting along, canoeing is the perfect way to enjoy this sparkling, clear stream. Just upstream from camp, Greer Spring pours 220 million gallons daily into the Eleven Point, so you'll have good river levels no matter how dry the season. The best stretch to float begins at Greer Crossing

CAMPGROUND RATINGS

Beauty: ★★★★★
Site privacy: ★★★★
Site spaciousness: ★★★★★
Quiet: ★★★★
Security: ★★★★
Cleanliness/upkeep: ★★★★★

A dip in the Eleven Point River is refreshing, but you'll be out in a hurry—most of its sparkling, clear water gushes from more than 30 springs along the stream, keeping the river cold on even the hottest summer day.

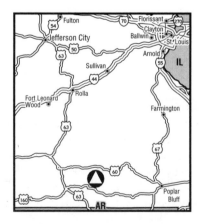

MARK TWAIN NATIONAL FOREST

and runs 19 miles to River-
ton. It's most enjoyable as a
two-day trip with an overnight at one of the six float
camps along the river.

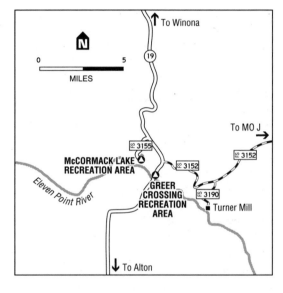

All the float camps are
nice, but White's Creek, located in the 16,500-acre Irish
Wilderness, is my favorite.
From the camp you can ex-
plore this remote wildland
on the White's Creek Trail.
A half-mile hike along the
south side of the loop goes
to White's Creek Cave, a
cool, 1,600-foot-long cavern
with many impressive for-
mations to admire as you
cool off from your walk. The cave is closed from September 15 through May 1 to
protect a hibernating colony of Indiana bats. Hiking 3 miles north from White's
Creek Camp, you'll meander through the woods to a quarter-mile section of
trail on a bluff above the Eleven Point leading to a spectacular overlook of Bliss
Spring that flows into the river.

If canoeing isn't your thing, there are plenty of great trails in the area. You
can hike the Irish Wilderness from Camp Five Pond Trailhead on MO J. From
the pond to White's Creek it's about 7 miles. You can hike or mountain bike
right from your campsite on the Ozark Trail. The Ozark Trail runs over 100
miles northeast from Greer Crossing, passing through the Ozark National
Scenic Riverways and extending all the way to Sutton Bluff Recreation Area.

Turner Mill Access is a haunting and historic spot on the Eleven Point. Accessible by either canoe or car, Turner Mill and Spring was once the location of
Surprise, a village named for the residents' reaction to approval of a post office
application for their remote village. The community was born in the 1850s
when G. W. Decker tapped a spring that flowed from a cave to power his mill

next to the Eleven Point. In 1891 Jesse L. Clay Turner bought the mill, refurbished it into a four-story structure, and operated it well into the 1900s. Turner also ran a general store, built a bridge over the river, provided land and materials for the Surprise School, and hired its teacher.

Little is left of Surprise today, but interpretive signs at the site tell the settlement's story and display a photo of the mill in its heyday. The spring still gurgles from a cave in the low bluff overlooking the mill site, and the 25-foot steel, overshot mill wheel, quiet for the last 60 years, stands like a ghost in the spring branch. Though you may have to push through the brush to get there, the Surprise School still stands in the woods 100 yards downriver, blackboard and outhouses still in place. Its last graduating class matriculated in 1945.

Turner Mill Access is 5 miles downriver by canoe or 11 miles by car on a combination of paved and gravel roads. Turner Mill makes a nice mountain bike ride, too. Pedal the Ozark Trail 10 miles east from Greer Crossing to the trailhead on FS 3152. Take FS 3152 a half mile east to FS 3190, then go south on FS 3190 to Turner Mill. A snack and a splash in the river at Turner Mill is the perfect boost for a return to Greer Crossing via roads for a 24-mile loop.

To get there: From Winona, take MO 19 south for 17 miles. The recreation area entrance is on the east side of the road just before the bridge over the Eleven Point River.

KEY INFORMATION

Greer Crossing Recreation Area
Mark Twain National Forest
Route 1, Box 1908
Winona, MO 65588

Operated by: U.S. Forest Service

Information: (573) 325-4233

Open: Year-round

Individual sites: 20

Each site has: Table, fire pit with grate, lantern pole; sites 9 and 13 have shelter roof over table

Site assignment: First come, first served

Registration: Self-registration at loop entrance

Facilities: Water, vault toilets, picnic area, river access, trails; water turned off November through March

Parking: At individual site

Fee: $8 per night

Elevation: 530 feet

Restrictions:

Pets—Allowed on leash

Fires—In fire grates

Alcoholic beverages—Allowed, subject to local ordinances

Vehicles—Up to 30 feet

Other—14-day stay limit; no glass containers within 50 feet of the river

LANE SPRING

Rolla, MO

L ane Spring Recreation Area is a pleasant little spot for an afternoon or weekend escape. Though it's close to the city of
Rolla, it's a hidden enclave in the valley of
Little Piney Creek that feels like the middle
of nowhere. Completely renovated in 1996,
the picnic area and campground are in
wonderful places to relax and enjoy the
outdoors.

The campground is well separated from
the beautiful, parklike picnic area, ensur-
ing a peaceful camping experience no matter how many day-users are in the park
area. Most sites are separated from their
neighbors by 100 feet or so, with thick
walls of trees and brush bolstering their
privacy. Many of the 18 campsites border
Little Piney Creek, with paths leading out
to the creek's gravel bars and cooling
water. The gurgling of the stream will lull
you to sleep by night and invite you to
drag your lawn chair and cold drink to its
shores by day. Tall pines and hardwoods
shade all of the sites.

Little Piney Creek, fed by numerous
springs, is a clear and chilly little stream.
Four of these springs—Lane, Yancy Mills,
Twin, and Table Rock—flow into the creek
near camp. Lane Spring, located in the picnic area, is a magical place. Stonework
walls, walks, and steps surround this little
bubbler and the branch that flows from the
spring over to Little Piney Creek. It's such
a beautiful spot that many couples from

CAMPGROUND RATINGS

Beauty:	★★★★
Site privacy:	★★★★
Site spaciousness:	★★★★
Quiet:	★★★★★
Security:	★★★★
Cleanliness/upkeep:	★★★★★

*Beautiful Lane Spring, with its
pretty spring and parklike setting,
is a popular place for weddings.*

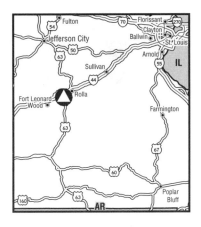

MARK TWAIN NATIONAL FOREST

Rolla and other surrounding towns come here for weddings and portraits.

From the stone overlook above Lane Spring, you can see the spring bubbling into the bottom of the pool. Fine silt dancing in the boils looks like delicate brown flowers or tiny volcanoes on the bottom of the pool and spring branch. Brilliant green watercress grows in the crystal clear spring water, adding vivid color to the scene even in winter.

Follow the stone steps to the water's edge where the

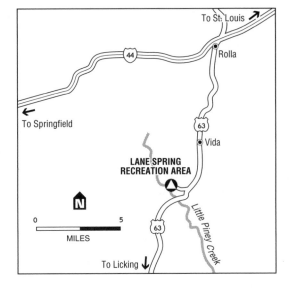

spring branch pours into Little Piney Creek. The spring-fed creek is a wonderful place to wade or swim on those hot and humid summer days in the Ozarks. Gravel bars, in-stream boulders, and cool, clear water make the creek a wonderful place to explore or just hang out enjoying nature's beauty.

Fly fishing is an excellent way to enjoy Little Piney Creek. Above and below Lane Spring Recreation Area, trout thrive in the cool water from the numerous springs feeding the Little Piney. In many places the creek is wide enough for backcasting, which makes it a good place for a novice fly fisher.

Even if you don't hook one, working your way up and down Little Piney Creek and letting your rod and reel pull you deeper into the outdoors is a fun way to spend an afternoon. I've often wondered who's getting caught—the fish by the fisherman, or the angler by the outdoors. Probably a little of both, just as it should be!

Hiking is another way to be pulled deeper into the outdoors at Lane Spring Recreation Area. Two trails built by Boy Scouts from Rolla explore the land above and along Little Piney Creek. The easier Cedar Bluff Trail covers 1.5 miles.

It begins next to the picnic area and climbs to a rocky glade near a bluff overlooking the valley of the creek. Bring your binoculars and enjoy the view, then follow the trail as it descends back to creek level and follows the bottomlands back to Lane Spring.

The 1-mile Blossom Rock Trail is a tougher hike but well worth your effort. You can start this hike behind the pay station or from a spur trail in the campground near sites 16 and 17. On this hike you'll climb high onto a bluff above Little Piney Creek and pass a huge sandstone boulder that gives the trail its name. This monster of a rock, 50 feet tall and 125 feet across, has cracks and lines that make its surface seem to blossom. From Blossom Rock the trail descends steeply to the bottoms, where you'll follow the creek back to the campground.

Other activities nearby include mountain biking and canoeing. Little Piney Creek flows into the Gasconade River not far from where its cousin, the Big Piney River, also joins the Gasconade. Both the Big Piney and the Gasconade are fine canoeing streams, with put-ins within 20–30 miles from Lane Spring. Just south of Newburg is the Kaintuck Trail, a network offering hiking and biking loops of 2–13 miles. Its trailhead is in Mill Creek Picnic Area, where another trout fishery thrives. You won't run out of things to do in this part of the Mark Twain National Forest.

To get there: From Rolla, drive 11 miles south on US 63 to FS 1892, where you'll see a sign for Lane Spring Recreation Area. Turn west and drive 1.4 miles to the recreation area. Turn left by the picnic area at the bottom of the hill and follow the signs a short distance to the campground.

KEY INFORMATION

Lane Spring Recreation Area
Mark Twain National Forest
401 Fairgrounds Road
Rolla, MO 65401

Operated by: U.S. Forest Service

Information: (573) 364-4501

Open: May 1–October 31

Individual sites: 17 single sites, 1 double

Each site has: Table, lantern pole, fire pit with grate

Site assignment: First come, first served; reservations available through National Recreation Reservation Service (877) 444-6777 or ReserveUSA.com

Registration: Self-pay at loop entrance

Facilities: Water, vault toilets, picnic area, pavilions, playground, trails

Parking: At individual site

Fee: $8 single site, $16 double, $25 pavilion rental, $2 per vehicle day-use fee; $8.65 fee for reservation (nonrefundable)

Elevation: 820 feet

Restrictions:

Pets—Allowed on leash

Fires—In fire pits

Alcoholic beverages—Allowed, subject to local ordinances

Vehicles—Up to 30 feet

Other—14-day stay limit, no glass containers in Little Piney Creek

L O G G E R S   L A K E

Bunker, MO

Loggers Lake is one of many beautiful facilities built throughout Missouri and Arkansas by the Great Depression–era Civilian Conservation Corps. Constructed in 1939–40 by CCC Company 1730 from nearby Bunker, Loggers Lake is a clear, blue 25-acre pool surrounded by green forested hills. The campground at this end-of-the-road hideaway is a peaceful Ozarks retreat.

Coming down the big hill to Loggers Lake, you first come to a pretty picnic area on a small peninsula to your right. Next you splash through the Mill Creek on a slab bridge, curve around the lake, pass another picnic area and the beach, and enter the campground. Sites 1–4 are above the beach and below the road. They're a bit close to the pavement, but being set 6 feet below road level makes them feel more secluded. Sites 5 and 6, down a short spur road right next to the lake, are very nice camping spots. All the first six sites are packed a little tightly together, but are well shaded and close to the beach.

Just beyond sites 1–6 the road enters the loop containing sites 7–14. These sites are farther apart and more spacious than sites 1–6. All sites except site 14 are on the outside of the loop with good distances between them. The loop is in a grassy open area with fewer trees than sites 1–6, giving each site a nice view of the lake. Sites 10–13 are closest to the water. Since the road is

CAMPGROUND RATINGS

Beauty:	★★★★
Site privacy:	★★★
Site spaciousness:	★★★★
Quiet:	★★★★
Security:	★★★★
Cleanliness/upkeep:	★★★★★

The gravel beach and open grassy lawn next to Loggers Lake are wonderful places for stargazing.

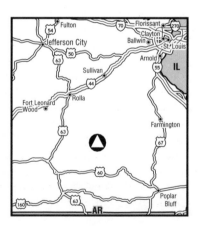

MARK TWAIN NATIONAL FOREST

paved, all sites are free of dust and that annoying rattle of tires on gravel.

This wonderful, laid-back campground is great for hanging out. Next to the picnic area is a small gravel beach perfect for swimming and wading. Loggers Lake is perfect for drifting around in your canoe, too. Whether from a canoe or the lake's shores, anglers can go after smallmouth bass and sunfish. The beach and the more open campsites in the loop make great places for soaking up some sun or doing a little late-night stargazing.

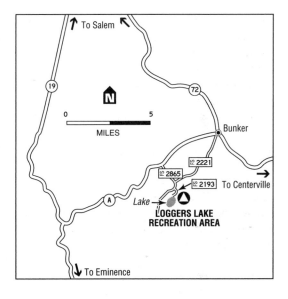

If you feel more active, you can hike two trails from the camp at Loggers Lake. A short 0.3-mile trail leads from the slab bridge over Mill Creek to Rock Springs, a small bubbler that helps Mill Creek keep the lake filled with cool water. A longer hike is the 1.5-mile Loggers Lake Nature Trail, a pretty tramp around the lakeshore. The trail starts behind site 13, where you'll find a trailhead and wooden sign with an etched route map. This loop hike crosses the dam, passes through tall oaks and pines, and has a spur to the now closed Oak Knoll Campground located on a ridge above the lake.

You can do some longer hiking and a bit of mountain biking on the nearby Ozark Trail, just 10 miles to the east. There's a trailhead 3 miles southeast of Bunker, at the junction of MO 72 and MO P. This trailhead is the southwestern end of the 18-mile Karkaghne Section of the Ozark Trail and the northern terminus of the 27-mile Blair Creek Section. The Karkaghne is open to mountain bikers and hikers, and its southwestern end offers the easiest bicycling on this section. You can make a nice 7-mile loop by riding from the trailhead east to

MO TT, passing through a huge grove of old-growth evergreens in Vest Hollow, then returning to the trailhead via MO TT and MO 72.

The Blair Creek Section parallels MO P, intersecting it 3 miles south of the trailhead. It follows a ridgetop between Blair and Big creeks with few difficult ups and downs. You can do a nice 6-mile loop by hiking the trail until it crosses MO P, then walking the little-traveled highway back to the trailhead. If you hike the entire Blair Creek Section of the Ozark Trail, you'll enjoy spectacular views at its southern end.

A short drive west takes you to the upper reaches of the Current River in the Ozark National Scenic Riverways. Loggers Lake is a nice base for exploration of the Ozark Riverways, as its campsites are inexpensive and uncrowded. At Akers Ferry, 25 miles west of Loggers Lake at the junction of MO K and MO KK, you can ride an old ferry across the upper Current River. You can also rent a canoe and check out this beautiful river from the seat of your boat.

To get there: From the MO 72/MO A junction in Bunker, drive 0.5 mile west on MO A to Lincoln Avenue, where a sign points southwest to Loggers Lake. Lincoln Avenue will change to gravel and become FS 2221. Follow Lincoln/FS 2221 6 miles to FS 2193. Turn south and go 1 mile to Loggers Lake.

Another unsigned route to the lake requires only 2 miles of gravel. Drive 5 miles southwest from Bunker on MO A to FS 2865 (look sharp—it's easy to miss this turn). Go 1 mile south on FS 2865 to FS 2221. Turn right and go 1 mile on FS 2221 to FS 2193. Turn south and go 1 mile to Loggers Lake.

KEY INFORMATION

Loggers Lake Recreation Area
Mark Twain National Forest
1301 S. Main Street
Salem, MO 65560

Operated by: U.S. Forest Service

Information: (573) 729-6656

Open: April 21–October 30

Individual sites: 14

Each site has: Table, fire pit with grate; most have lantern pole

Site assignment: First come, first served

Registration: Self-pay station at campground entrance

Facilities: Water, vault toilets, picnic area, swimming beach, boat ramp, horseshoe pits, trail

Parking: At individual site

Fee: $8 per site, $2 per vehicle for day use

Elevation: 1,020 feet

Restrictions:

Pets—Allowed on leash

Fires—In fire pits

Alcoholic beverages—Allowed but subject to local ordinances

Vehicles—Up to 25 feet

Other—14-day stay limit; no glass containers on swimming beach

MARBLE CREEK

Ironton, MO

CAMPGROUND RATINGS

Marble Creek is named for the pinkish dolomite called taum sauk marble. This marble is found along the creek's 20-mile course through the surrounding St. Francois Mountains. Like so many Ozark streams, the creek was once harnessed to power a mill. In Marble Creek Recreations Area you can swim in the old mill pool and examine crumbling foundations of a mill that last operated in the 1930s.

The campground is nestled into a horse-shoe bend of Marble Creek with a pleasant blend of thick woods and open tree cover. Sites on the back half of the loop are farther apart and are separated by thick bands of brush, while those near the front of the campground are more open and parklike. Head for the back of the loop for the most privacy and peace and to the front sites for an open atmosphere and grassy camping areas. Several sites on the east side of the loop are set back in the trees, with small grassy meadows opening up behind them. At Marble Creek Campground there's a site to please almost anyone.

The picnic area and the millpond are west of the campground loop. The pool is deep, clear, and inviting. Rocks for sunbathing are everywhere up and down this rugged little creek. Bring your rod and reel—smallmouth and rock bass can be caught in the millpond and other pools along Marble Creek. The creek is especially beautiful in spring, when heavier flows make this little stream rush

Beauty: ★★★★
Site privacy: ★★★★
Site spaciousness: ★★★★★
Quiet: ★★★★
Security: ★★★★
Cleanliness/upkeep: ★★★★★

The pond behind the old milldam on Marble Creek is sparkling, clear, and inviting.

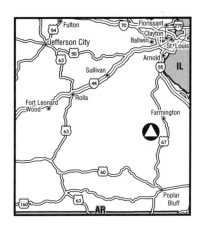

MARK TWAIN NATIONAL FOREST

and ripple, lulling you to sleep each evening.

A trailhead for the Ozark Trail lies at the campground entrance. The Marble Creek Section of the Ozark Trail takes off across MO E to the southwest and runs 8 miles to Crane Lake. Open to both hikers and mountain bikers, this trail is a good introduction to the St. Francois Mountains around Marble Creek. It alternately climbs to scenic ridgetops and descends into cool, wooded hollows. Halfway to Crane Lake the trail meanders through a set of rugged, rocky glades with fine vistas of the surrounding mountains.

Upon reaching Crane Lake, the Ozark Trail connects to the 5-mile Crane Lake Trail built by the forest service and the Youth Conservation Corps in the 1970s. The trail around the lake is divided into a 3-mile northern loop and a 2-mile southern loop, with the dam as the cutoff route. This scenic trail follows the lake's edge in some places and climbs to blue-water vistas in others. Below the dam, Crane Pond Creek rushes through a beautiful series of shut-ins, pools, and waterfalls in Reader Hollow. Near the junction of the two trails, a little spring gurgles from the rocks and joins Crane Pond Creek.

If you bike to Crane Lake, it's easy to turn the ride into a loop by returning to Marble Creek via gravel roads and MO E. Ride 2 miles north on the gravel road leading north from the lake, and turn right at the intersection there. Follow that road 2.5 miles to MO E, then turn right on MO E and proceed 4 miles to Marble Creek. If you're driving from Marble Creek to Crane to shuttle hikers or pick up cyclists, just reverse the directions. There will be a sign on MO E directing you to Crane Lake.

Crane is a national forest picnic site, with tables scattered in the woods next to the lake. It's fun to go to Crane and hike the trail and enjoy a picnic. Bring your fishing pole—the lake is stocked with bass, sunfish, and catfish. Maybe you can catch your supper there!

Other attractions in the area include the Crane Mountain Lookout 8 miles northwest of the campsite, and Taum Sauk Mountain State Park 20 miles to the southwest. At Taum Sauk Mountain, the highest point in Missouri, you can climb a fire lookout on top of this 1,772-foot peak (see more about Taum Sauk Mountain State Park in the profile on page 18).

(see more about Taum Sauk Mountain State Park in the profile on page 18).

To get there: Drive 2 miles south of Fredericktown on US 67 to MO E. Turn west on MO E and drive 18 miles to Marble Creek Recreation Area.

KEY INFORMATION

**Marble Creek Campground
Mark Twain National Forest
P.O. Box 188
Potosi, MO 63664**

Operated by: U.S. Forest Service

Information: (573) 438-5427

Open: May 1–October 30

Individual sites: 25

Each site has: Table, fire pit with grate, lantern pole

Site assignment: First come, first served; reservations available through National Recreation Reservation Service (877) 444-6777 or ReserveUSA.com

Registration: Self-pay at loop entrance

Facilities: Vault toilets, swimming hole, trails

Parking: At individual site

Fee: $8 single site, $16 double, $2 per vehicle day-use areas; $8.65 fee for reservation (nonrefundable)

Elevation: 660 feet

Restrictions:

Pets—Allowed on leash

Fires—In fire pits

Alcoholic beverages—Allowed, subject to local ordinances

Vehicles—Up to 25 feet

Other—14-day stay limit; no glass containers near swimming hole or creek

MARKHAM SPRING

Williamsville, MO

If you like water, you'll love Markham Spring. A deep, clear, spring-fed pool with an old home and a mill house on its shores is the centerpiece of the recreation area. Little brooks trickle everywhere near the pond and picnic area, flowing from the pool and a couple of small springs in this pretty valley. If you want your streams a little bigger, the Black River flows along the backside of the campground loops. Two and a half miles of scenic trails are great for showing you around the pretty hideaway next to the Black River.

The campground's four loops are named Pine, Sycamore, River, and Birch. Pine Loop, containing sites 1–12, is on your right as you drive along the campground road. All its sites are very nice, but the pick camping spot is site 6. It's right next to the Black River. Sites 13–26 are in Sycamore Loop, the next set of campsites along the park road. Sycamore is a mirror image of Pine Loop, with shady, level, well-spaced sites separated by thin curtains of brush. Site 18, closest to the Black River with a view of the stream, is the best site in Sycamore Loop.

Though it's called River Loop, the third cluster, containing sites 30–44, isn't really any closer to the river than Pine and Sycamore Loops. Most of its sites are nice, but sites 41–44 are a little crowded and too close to the road. Preferred spots in the River Loop are sites 37 and 39 next to the river. Site 40 is another good one, set on a lit-

CAMPGROUND RATINGS

Beauty:	★★★★★
Site privacy:	★★★★
Site spaciousness:	★★★★
Quiet:	★★★★
Security:	★★★★
Cleanliness/upkeep:	★★★★★

If water soothes your soul, you'll love the springs, brooks, millpond, and river at Markham Spring Recreation Area.

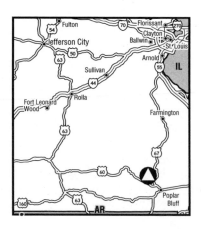

MARK TWAIN NATIONAL FOREST

tle bench above the road beneath a low bluff. Birch Loop at the end of the park road contains three group sites, which are scattered along the edge of an open area and have a few shade trees.

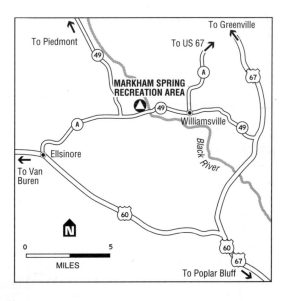

Markham Springs Recreation Area is a wonderful woodland hang-out. The picturesque valley's scenery is best enjoyed on a leisurely walk from your campsite. The stone home next to the millpond was built in the 1930s and got its electricity from a mill wheel powered by the pool's outflow. The mill house and water wheel still stand at the south end of the pond. Paths and bridges spanning the brooks make for delightful exploration of the area south of the spring pool.

Near the pond you'll find Bubble Spring, a small trickle gurgling from the earth and feeding a small stream. Little boils of sand in the bottom of a clear pool mark the spring's outflow. South of the spring and millpond is Island Picnic Area, a beautifully shaded narrow tract of land between two spring branches. Island is a wonderful place to read, write, or nap on a blanket in the grass.

It's a nice hike on the Eagle Bluff Trail onto the ridge above camp, where you'll enjoy the view of the Black River Valley. The trail starts near the boat launch and climbs high above Markham Spring on rough steps, then follows the ridge north. Halfway along the ridgeline you can shorten your hike by taking a cut-off trail leading down to the millpond. If you continue north, you'll eventually descend to river level and follow the stream back to the campground in Sycamore Loop. There you can pick up the River Trail and follow it all the way downstream to the boat launch.

If you're feeling really energetic, load up your mountain bike before heading to Markham Spring. Four nearby trails, all within easy drives of the campground, offer 85 miles of knobby-tired fun. Just a few miles to the south is the 22-mile Victory Section of the Ozark Trail. It's a point-to-point ride that can be made into a loop by combining sections of trail with gravel forest roads.

The southern trailhead for the Lake Wappapello Section of the Ozark Trail is 12 miles away on MO 172 just east of US 67. Of its 31-mile length, the southernmost 15 miles offer the easiest riding. This trail has a connector to the Lake Wappapello Trail in Lake Wappapello State Park, a 15-mile loop ride along the lakeshore and through the hills and hollows to the lake's west.

The Lake Wappapello Trail in turn connects to the University Forest Trail, an 18-mile loop through the University Forest Conservation Area. This ride is the easiest and most fun of the four trails in the area. Five road crossings allow short loop options if you don't feel up to the whole distance, and you'll love the 5 miles of narrow, twisting single-track on the stretch of trail south of MO KK. For more detailed information on these trails, pick up a copy of *Mountain Bike! The Ozarks, A Guide to the Classic Trails*, written by Steve Henry (see the Bibliography on page 168). It'll show you where the trails are, help you decide which is right for your skills, and show you the various distance options on each ride.

To get there: From Williamsville, drive 3 miles west on MO 49. The entrance will be on the north side of the road, just after you cross the Black River. The campground is at the back of the recreation area.

KEY INFORMATION

Markham Spring Recreation Area
Mark Twain National Forest
1420 Maud, P.O. Box 988
Poplar Bluff, MO 63901

Operated by: U.S. Forest Service

Information: (573) 785-1475

Open: May 27–October 15

Individual sites: 40 single sites, 4 double, 3 group

Each site has: Table, fire pit with grate, lantern pole

Site assignment: First come, first served

Registration: Self-pay at campground entrance

Facilities: Water, showers, flush toilets, dump station, picnic area, river access, horseshoe pits, volleyball net, trails

Parking: At individual site

Fee: $8 single site, $16 double; group sites $25 for up to 25 people; $2 per vehicle for day-use

Elevation: 400 feet

Restrictions:

Pets—Allowed on leash

Fires—In fire pits

Alcoholic beverages—Allowed, subject to local ordinances

Vehicles—Up to 50 feet

Other—14-day stay limit; no swimming in spring pools and streams; no glass bottles in river

McCORMACK LAKE

Winona, MO

Set next to a 15-acre lake built by the Civilian Conservation Corps, McCormack Lake Recreation Area is a quiet and relaxing hideaway. While McCormack isn't spectacular like many of the campgrounds in the Ozarks, it's a peaceful, comfortable place at the end of the road. Since McCormack has only eight sites, it doesn't get crowded and noisy, yet it's only a short distance from the Eleven Point River and its great canoeing and fishing. McCormack Lake itself offers pretty good angling, and great hiking and mountain biking trails leave right from your campsite. It's a free camp, too—one of the last good deals in the outdoors!

Only six of McCormack's eight sites are regularly used. Sites 1 and 2 are not level, so their tables are usually appropriated and moved to more suitable campsites. Sites 4 and 5 next to the water are the primo spots at McCormack Lake. All sites are grassy and shaded by large trees. In this small, open campground under the trees, you can see all your neighbors, but adequate distances between sites keep the place from seeming crowded. You can get water at a spigot in the picnic area across the lake, but a notice on the faucet warns that it should be boiled or purified.

McCormack Lake is great for hikers and bikers. For warm-ups or quick sunrise and sunset walks, there is a quarter-mile trail around the lake. For the more energetic,

CAMPGROUND RATINGS

Beauty:	★★★★
Site privacy:	★★★
Site spaciousness:	★★★★
Quiet:	★★★★★
Security:	★★★★
Cleanliness/upkeep:	★★★★

While you're camping out in Eleven Point River country, make sure you don't miss hiking to the incomparable Greer Spring.

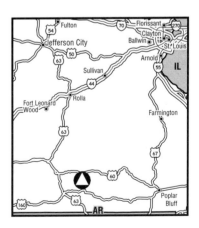

MARK TWAIN NATIONAL FOREST

there's the 3.7-mile McCormack-Greer Trail. From the dam it follows McCormack Hollow down to the Eleven Point River and joins the Ozark Trail. It then climbs onto a bluff nearly 300 feet above the river to the Boomhole View, which provides grand vistas up and down this National Wild and Scenic River. During turn-of-the-century logging days, a wooden chute on the bluff across the river was used to slide huge logs down to the Eleven Point, where they landed in the stream with a loud, booming splash.

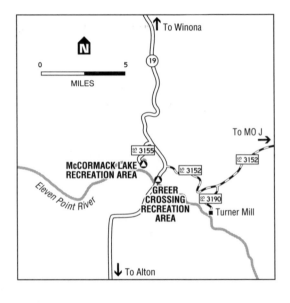

From the Boomhole the trail descends into Duncan Hollow and forks. Both options go to Greer Crossing, but the left fork climbs onto and follows a ridge above the Eleven Point, while the easier right trail hugs the riverbank. On the river trail you'll see Greer Spring Branch pouring into the Eleven Point, more than doubling the river's size.

Greer Spring, from which the branch flows, is a must-see. A 1-mile trail leads to this natural wonder. To take this hike, drive 1.5 miles south of Greer Crossing on MO 19 to a trailhead on the west side of the road. Greer is the second-largest spring in Missouri, gushing 220 million gallons daily into the Eleven Point. From a beautiful stone overlook you'll admire the deep blue-green boil of the main spring to your right and a smaller flow emanating from Greer Spring Cave to your left. No matter how hot the day, it's always cool down next to the spring and its 55-degree outflow.

The natural beauty of Greer Spring and the surrounding forest make it hard to picture this spot as a beehive of activity in the late 1800s. Samuel Greer first built a mill at the spring in 1860. As the forest was logged and farms sprung up in the area, the mill used Greer Spring's power to saw lumber, grind corn, and gin cotton. In 1883 Greer built a new dam and rebuilt the mill on the hilltop north of the spring, using a cable system to transmit power from the wheel at the spring to the mill above.

The mill finally shut down in 1920, and two years later the Dennig family purchased the spring and the land around it. The Dennigs took incredibly good care of the spring for 70 years, and then sold it in the late 1980s. The Mark Twain National Forest acquired this natural gem in 1993 through an Anheuser-Busch grant to the River Network and money donated by conservationist Leo Drey. Until 2013, the Dennig family has control of the 110 acres near the spring, where the old mill still stands. Please do not trespass on their land while checking out the spring.

Another attraction near McCormack Lake is Falling Spring Picnic Area. To get there, drive 3 miles north of McCormack Lake on MO 19 to FS 3164. Go east on FS 3164, taking the left fork just off the highway, and drive 2 miles to the picnic area. Falling Spring pours 500,000 gallons per day from a rock wall to a pool 50 feet below. You'll also see ruins of another of the old mills that were once liberally scattered throughout the Ozarks. (See the Greer Crossing profile on page 48 for still more trails and attractions in the Eleven Point River country.)

To get there: From Winona, drive 13 miles south on MO 19 to Forest Road 3155. Turn right on FS 3155 and drive 2 miles to the recreation area.

KEY INFORMATION

McCormack Lake Recreation Area
Mark Twain National Forest
Route 1, Box 1908
Winona, MO 65588

Operated by: U.S. Forest Service

Information: (573) 325-4233

Open: Year-round

Individual sites: 8

Each site has: Table, lantern pole, fire pit with grate

Site assignment: First come, first served

Registration: No registration required

Facilities: Vault toilets; water faucet in picnic area, boil or purification order in effect

Parking: At individual site

Fee: No fee

Elevation: 600 feet

Restrictions:

Pets—Allowed on leash

Fires—In fire pits

Alcoholic beverages—Allowed, subject to local ordinances

Vehicles—Up to 20 feet

Other—14-day stay limit

NORTH FORK

Dora, MO

Known to locals as Hammond Mill Camp, North Fork Recreation Area overlooks another of Missouri's many cool, clear, spring-fed streams—the North Fork of the White River. A pretty spring pours into the river a short hike from the far end of the campground. The picnic area and river access are at the far end of camp, where a low bluff overlooks the perfect spot for a swim during the dog days of an Ozarks summer. The 6,600-acre Devil's Backbone Wilderness wraps around camp to the east, south, and west, and the Ridge Runner Trail heads north from the trailhead near the picnic area. Whether you hike, mountain bike, canoe, or just hang out—you can be as busy or as lazy as you want in this Ozarks haven.

The campground is laid out in three loops hanging like tadpoles off the main road. The sites on the tail of the tadpole are most private, while those on the turnaround that forms the tadpole's head are a little closer together. The first of these is Dogwood Loop, sites 1–6, with the campground host in site 1. Sites 7–14 are in Willow Loop. With the most sites of the three loops, Willow is a little crowded, but trees separate most sites. Pine Loop is the farthest from the entrance, with sites 15–20. Site 20, at the end of Pine Loop with a view of the river, is the best spot in the campground.

Just past the Pine Loop is the trailhead for the quarter-mile hike to Blue Spring.

CAMPGROUND RATINGS

Beauty: ★★★★★
Site privacy: ★★★★
Site spaciousness: ★★★★
Quiet: ★★★★
Security: ★★★★
Cleanliness/upkeep: ★★★★★

From North Fork Campground you can explore the 6,600-acre Devil's Backbone Wilderness by hiking or canoeing into deep hills and hollows.

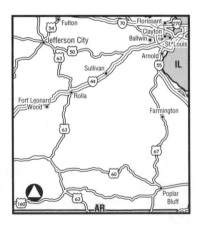

MARK TWAIN NATIONAL FOREST

With an average flow of seven million gallons per day, it's not huge like Greer or Alley springs, but this exquisite, blue-green pool a few feet from the North Fork is still an Ozark gem. My friend Janet, who grew up in nearby West Plains, used to bring unsuspecting friends to the campground to go tubing. As they floated downriver she'd lure them to the riverside next to the spring, just to hear them gasp and squeal as they drifted unknowingly into the cold outflow.

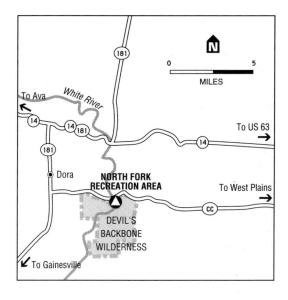

The spring trail is nice, following the river's edge on the way out to Blue Spring and climbing gently onto hillsides above the stream on the return to the trailhead. It meanders past fascinating rock outcroppings, along ledges, and over old stone steps and bridges, with benches along the way for relaxing at the scenic spots. At the spring it skirts the pool's edge, where you can admire the gently roiling surface, and then climbs on top of a small bluff above the spring so you can peer into the blue-green depths. My favorite view is from the short trail running downriver 100 feet from the overlook, where there's a nice vista of the North Fork winding into the forested hills of the Devil's Backbone Wilderness.

You can explore Devil's Backbone from the Blue Spring Trail. Looping back to camp uphill behind the spring, you'll see a trail breaking off to the south. Follow this path a quarter mile uphill onto McGarr Ridge, and you'll intersect one of the trails that wander through this pretty wilderness area. Turn right, and the trail descends over the next mile to a scenic bend in the North Fork. From there, you can swing south and east to follow the trail up Crooked Creek, with optional side trips to McGarr Spring to the north and the Devil's Backbone, a steep-sided narrow ridge, to the south. The trail eventually meanders around the north part of the wilderness, passes a spur leading to a trailhead on MO CC east of the campground, and returns to the Blue Spring spur for a very scenic 9-mile loop.

The Ridge Runner Trail, open to both hikers and mountain bikers, leaves the campground to the north from the trail-head between the camp and the picnic area. On the map it looks like a barbell, with a southern loop near the camp-ground, and a long connector going north to another loop at Noblett Lake Recreation area. The Noblett Loop is 8 miles long and is more rugged than the southern loop. It's a great hike but a difficult mountain bike ride.

The 12-mile North Fork Loop, north of the campground, offers a pleasant hike through wooded hills and is a good intermediate mountain bike ride. I like the west side of the trail best. It hugs the river in a quarter-mile stretch and climbs up high above the North Fork for some nice views of the North Fork valley. When you're next to the North Fork, keep an eye out for river otters—they were recently reintroduced here and are doing well.

When you tire of hiking, rent a tube or canoe and float the beautiful North Fork of the White River. Twin Bridges to the North Fork Campground is an easy 5-mile float. If you paddle 4 miles past camp to North Fork Spring, bring your fly rod—you'll be in trout waters for the next 12 miles.

To get there: Go 16 miles west of West Plains on MO CC. North Fork Recreation Area is on the south side of the highway, right before MO CC crosses the North Fork of the White River.

KEY INFORMATION

**North Fork Recreation Area
Mark Twain National Forest
906 Old Springfield Road
Willow Springs, MO 65793**

Operated by: U.S. Forest Service

Information: (417) 469-3155

Open: May 15–December 1

Individual sites: 20

Each site has: Table, fire pit with grate, lantern pole, cooking shelter

Site assignment: First come, first served

Registration: Self-pay at camp-ground entrance

Facilities: Water, vault toilets, picnic area, phone, river access, trails; water turned off October 15

Parking: At individual site

Fee: $8 per site, $2 per vehicle in day-use area

Elevation: 700 feet

Restrictions:

  Pets—Allowed on leash

  Fires—In fire pits

  Alcoholic beverages—Allowed, subject to local ordinances

  Vehicles—Up to 30 feet

  Other—14-day stay limit

PADDY CREEK

Licking, MO

Paddy Creek Recreation Area isn't just another nice campground—it's my favorite Missouri camping spot. I love Paddy Creek's beauty, but fun memories make it special for me, too. I'll never forget waking in pre-dawn darkness one April morning and hearing a low voice from the next site murmur, "I've got a shotgun, you've got a shotgun, he's got a shotgun . . . I guess we're ready to go." I chuckled in my sleeping bag, thankful I knew it was turkey season.

Spending a few nights at Paddy Creek might put this campground at the top of your list, too. Tall bluffs overlook Paddy Creek as it curves around the campground to join the Big Piney River to the east. The campground is at the end of the road into the recreation area, so it's remote and quiet. A cooling splash in Paddy Creek is less than 200 feet from all sites. Distance between the sites is good, and all except site 23 are well shaded. Even so, I really like site 23. One tree shades its table, and an open grassy area stretches north of it. It's well suited for several tents, and its grassy field is perfect for Frisbee, sunbathing, or stargazing. Sites 14 and 15 are the best sites at Paddy Creek, overlooking the stream at the end of the campground road.

A terrific campground for hikers, Paddy Creek is located at the eastern edge of the 7,000-acre Paddy Creek Wilderness Area. The Big Paddy and Little Paddy creeks meander through the wilderness area. You can

CAMPGROUND RATINGS

Beauty:	★★★★★
Site privacy:	★★★★★
Site spaciousness:	★★★★
Quiet:	★★★★★
Security:	★★★★
Cleanliness/upkeep:	★★★★★

Paddy Creek Recreation Area is perfect for hikers. You can explore the 7,000-acre Paddy Creek Wilderness on the 17-mile Big Piney Trail.

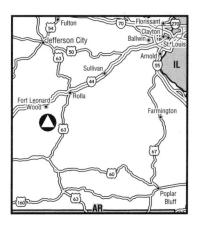

MARK TWAIN NATIONAL FOREST

explore the hills and hollows around these creeks on the 17-mile Big Piney Trail. A cut-off divides this long and narrow loop into two sections, making it perfect for weekend hikers. You can hike the east half of the wilderness on a Saturday ramble of around 12 miles and poke around the west half on a 9-mile jaunt on Sunday. Maps are at the pay station in the campground. Maps and trail signs for the wilderness are confusing, referring to a South Loop and a North Loop. They really refer to the north and south sides of the Big Piney Trail. These two sides meet near Roby Lake Picnic Area, trail-head for hiking the west half of the Big Piney Trail.

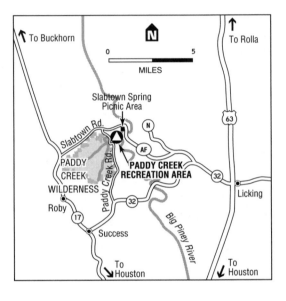

You can hike the east half of the Big Piney right from your campsite. Don't bother to walk to the trailhead—just cross the creek next to the camp, push about 100 feet through the woods and turn right onto the north-side trail. Just over a mile later you'll be enjoying a beautiful overlook of the campground and the hills to the south—a wonderful place to watch the sunset. A half mile farther is the Big Piney Trail Camp, designed for equestrians. With picnic tables in a grove of pines, it's a great place for a meal. Three miles into your hike the trail crosses Forest Road 220. For an easy 5-mile loop, you can turn left here and follow the road back to camp.

West of FS 220 the trail enters the wilderness. About 1 mile in you'll cross a stream that's usually dry. About a quarter mile down this wash is a beautiful little box canyon and spring. Another mile past the spring is the cut-off that cuts 1 mile across the loop to the south side of the Big Piney Trail, where a left turn heads toward the campground. The cut-off crosses Little Paddy Creek, so in spring you might get wet feet. About a half mile before reaching camp you'll get wet again, this time crossing Big Paddy Creek in a pretty bottomland just west of camp.

Don't blow off the west half of the Big Piney Trail from Roby Lake, especially in spring, when the creeks are flowing strongly. Three miles along the south side the trail hugs several hundred yards of steep cliffs overlooking the headwaters of Little Paddy Creek. This vista faces southeast, so it's a wonderful place for a snack or napping in the morning sun. On the north side, 2.5 miles east of the trailhead, there's a rocky streambed with ledges and cascades. When the creek is flowing, an exquisite little waterfall pours off an 8-foot undercut ledge. The waterfall's undercut is so deep that you can scramble underneath and admire the wilderness through a sparkling curtain of water.

Two short trails in the area are worth a look, too. The 1-mile Paddy Creek Trail starts at the picnic area and explores the creek banks to the west. Its best feature is a spectacular overlook, complete with benches and boulders for watching the sunset. The other short hike is the 1.5-mile Slabtown Bluff Trail at nearby Slabtown Bluff Picnic Area, a few miles to the east. It follows the Big Piney River, then climbs to a bluff overlook with beautiful vistas.

To get there: Drive 13 miles west from Licking on MO 32 to Paddy Creek Road (FS 220). Turn right and follow this gravel road 6 miles to Paddy Creek Recreation Area. Turn right into Paddy Creek and drive through the picnic area, past the trailhead, and into the campground at the end of the road. To reach Roby Lake Picnic Area and the west trailhead for the Big Piney Trail, drive 1 mile north from Roby on MO 17 to FS 274, then go east a half mile to Roby Lake.

KEY INFORMATION

Paddy Creek Recreation Area
Mark Twain National Forest
108 Sam Houston Boulevard
Houston, MO 65483

Operated by: U.S. Forest Service

Information: (417) 967-4194

Open: April 1–November 30; camping permitted in picnic area December 1–March 31

Individual sites: 23

Each site has: Table, lantern pole, fire pit with grate

Site assignment: First come, first served

Registration: Self-pay at campground entrance

Facilities: Vault toilets, picnic area, trails; bring your own water

Parking: At individual site

Fee: $5

Elevation: 890 feet

Restrictions:

Pets—Allowed on leash

Fires—In fire pits

Alcoholic beverages—Allowed, subject to local ordinances

Vehicles—Up to 30 feet

Other—14-day stay limit

RED BLUFF RECREATION AREA

Davisville, MO

R ed Bluff Recreation Area is a beautiful forested enclave in a horseshoe bend of Huzzah Creek. The campground takes its name from the red hues in the cliff across the Huzzah. The light rusty color results from oxidization of iron compounds in the rock strata. Indians called the bluff "Painted Rock."

It seems that every streamside campground in the Ozarks was once a mill site, and Red Bluff Recreation Area is no exception. Two different mills once operated on the Huzzah in the 1800s. Boyer Mill, built around 1830 near the downstream campground, was the first. Bryant's Mill followed about 30 years later. A community named Boyer grew around the site. Over time, the community's center moved a short distance downstream and was renamed Davisville.

Though the campground is only a mile from the village of Davisville, it feels like it's in the middle of nowhere—in other words, it's a wonderful place. This pretty streamside getaway is divided into three loops. Sites 1–23 are in Bryant Mill Loop, where the old gristmill once operated. Though there are nice sites in this loop, it has the least shade and privacy, some sites are close together, and the ground is somewhat rocky. The loop is very close to the creek, so if access to the stream is important to you, this is the place to be. Site 7 is closest to the Huzzah. Sites 13, 16, and 18 are the

CAMPGROUND RATINGS

Beauty:	★★★★★
Site privacy:	★★★
Site spaciousness:	★★★★
Quiet:	★★★★
Security:	★★★
Cleanliness/upkeep:	★★★★★

Admire the red bluff towering over Huzzah Creek from your campsite at the Pines Overlook.

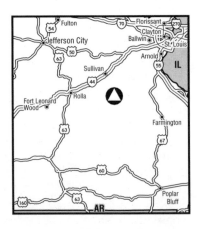

MARK TWAIN NATIONAL FOREST

nicest sites on the Bryant Mill Loop.

Sites 24–43 are set downstream, where the Boyer Mill once stood. Scattered along a tadpole-shaped loop, these grassy sites provide better shade and spacing and are more private. Sites 24–37 are along the tadpole's tail, and 38–43 are on the turnaround loop at the end of the road. My favorite spot on this loop is site 30. It's a double site with a grassy field stretching behind it to Huzzah Creek. The group sites are east of this field. They are some of the best group sites in the Ozarks.

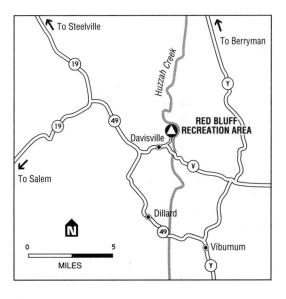

The last three sites are the best sites at Red Bluff. A quarter mile down the entrance road, a sign on the right points to the Pines Overlook. Sites 44, 45, and 46 are in a pine grove there. Site 44 is in the woods, 100 feet from the edge of a cliff. It's a nice spot, but sites 45 and 46, the best sites in Red Bluff and quite possibly the two coolest campsites in Missouri, sit smack on the edge of a bluff over the wooded Huzzah Valley. With only three sites, it won't ever be crowded at the overlook. It's always a quiet place where the only sound is the breeze sighing through the pines. If you do want to visit the main campground, it's only a short walk down the Red Bluff Trail that goes by the overlook on its way to the main campground. Unless you sleepwalk or fear heights, try for one of these three sites.

The Red Bluff Trail starts at the picnic area parking lot. It's a nice one-mile loop through the forest above camp, past the Pines Overlook, and back to the picnic area. It's open to both hikers and mountain bikers and is suitable for novices. Another easy trail starts near the picnic area and follows the Huzzah a half mile upstream past the Red Bluff.

Huzzah Creek is the big attraction at Red Bluff Recreation Area. It has nice swimming and wading areas and is a fun tubing run through the campground. Tubes can be rented or purchased from the campground hosts. They also sell ice, wood, and minimal camping and fishing supplies. Bring your rod and reel and go after the smallmouth and rock bass lurking in the Huzzah.

Huzzah Creek is more than a tubing and fishing stream—it's also a fine canoe run. The creek flows 23 miles from the MO V bridge near the campground to the confluence with the Meramec River. It is a pretty float all the way. In dry seasons near Red Bluff, water levels may be too low, but from MO 8 to the Meramec it's usually floatable year-round. More canoeing fun is on Courtois Creek, which parallels the Huzzah a few miles to the north. The Courtois dumps into the Huzzah a bit south of the Meramec River.

Great road biking can be found on the hilly, empty highways around Davisville. The roads also allow for wonderful scenic drives, especially during October, when fall colors peak, or in spring, when the dogwoods bloom. On your drive go to Dillard Mill State Historic Site on MO 49 and tour one of the best-preserved gristmills in the Ozarks. For mountain bikers, the Berryman Trail, thought by many to be the best ride in the state, is 15 miles to the north. Tubing, canoeing, biking, hiking, bird-watching, or just listening to the wind that whispers in the pines—there's something for everyone at Red Bluff Recreation Area.

To get there: From Davisville, drive 1 mile east on MO V, then turn left into Red Bluff Recreation Area.

KEY INFORMATION

**Red Bluff Recreation Area
Mark Twain National Forest
P.O. Box 188
Potosi, MO 63664**

Operated by: U.S. Forest Service

Information: (573) 438-5427

Open: May 1–October 15

Individual sites: 39 single sites, 7 double, 3 group

Each site has: Table, fire pit with grate, lantern pole; some sites have cooking shelters

Site assignment: First come, first served; reservations available through National Recreation Reservation Service (877) 444-6777 or ReserveUSA.com

Registration: Self-pay at entrance station

Facilities: Water, vault toilets, picnic area, pavilion, trail, swimming hole

Parking: At individual site

Fee: $8 single, $16 double, $25 group; $8.65 (nonrefundable) reservation fee; pavilion $25; $2 per vehicle day-use fee

Elevation: 800 feet

Restrictions:

Pets—Allowed on leash

Fires—In fire pits

Alcoholic beverages—Allowed, subject to local ordinances

Vehicles—Up to 40 feet

Other—14-day stay limit; no glass containers in Huzzah Creek

SILVER MINES

Fredericktown, MO

Silver Mines Recreation Area is one of the most beautiful spots in Missouri. It's a shame this campground isn't open year-round. This is where the St. Francis River cuts a rugged canyon through granite bluffs overlooking its rocky course through the mountains. At the turn of the century, the Ozark hills surrounding Silver Mines were part of a busy mining district of the forest. One reminder of those days is an old mill site and dam built by the Einstein Mining Company for processing ore for silver, lead, and other minerals. Located upstream from the bridge on County Road D, the now-breached dam is one of the many rapids enjoyed by kayakers and canoeists on the St. Francis, Missouri's only whitewater river.

Now the miners are gone, their place taken by visitors to this popular recreation site in the Mark Twain National Forest. Silver Mines encompasses four campground loops, two picnic areas, a boulder-studded swimming hole, boater access sites, river trails, and lots of rapids and scenery.

Riverside Loop is located just south of the bridge over the St. Francis. It offers 12 sites next to the river, scattered on both sides of a loop road around a small grassy open area. This is where you'll find the campground host. It's also the best place for swimmers to camp, because it's next to the picnic area and swimming hole parking area. Only a few hundred feet down the road is the old

CAMPGROUND RATINGS

Beauty:	★★★★★
Site privacy:	★★★★★
Site spaciousness:	★★★★★
Quiet:	★★★★★
Security:	★★★★
Cleanliness/upkeep:	★★★★★

The wild St. Francis River upstream from Silver Mines Campground is one of the most scenic places in Missouri.

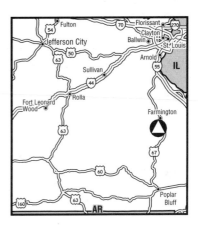

MARK TWAIN NATIONAL FOREST

MO D low-water bridge, re-placed only a few years ago by a modern span downstream.

Just across the river to the north are Summit Loop, with 25 sites, and Prospect Loop, with 18 sites. Located side by side on a wooded hill above the river, they are breezier, better shaded, and offer better site spacing and privacy than Riverside. They are a bit farther from the St. Francis than Riverside but are cooler and more secluded.

Spring Branch Loop is a half mile north of Prospect and Summit. Serving as overflow camping when the other three loops are full, Spring Branch opens only on those few spring weekends when early season rains transform the St. Francis River into a whitewater paradise, attracting paddlers from all over Missouri and Arkansas. It isn't as well kept or level as the other loops, but it's built in a grove of large pine and hardwood trees that sigh in the breeze. More secluded and peaceful than the other loops, it's my favorite of the four loops at Silver Mines.

Hiking and boating are the best ways to enjoy Silver Mines. You'll need whitewater skills to run the river, though. Beginning upstream at the MO 72 Bridge, the St. Francis River challenges boaters with rapids named Land of Oz, Big Drop, Cat's Paw, Double-Drop, and Rickety Rack. Each March the Missouri Whitewater Championships are held in Millstream Gardens Conservation Area, 2 miles upstream from the campgrounds.

At Millstream the river crashes through the Tiemann Shut-Ins, creating rapids that draw for the races boaters from all over the eastern half of the United States. With huge boulders in the river and on the hillside that slopes downward from the north side of the stream, Millstream is the perfect place to watch the competition and admire the spectacular rock garden in the riverbed. When graced by nice spring weather, race weekends attract as many as 2,000 spectators who relax on the boulders and enjoy picnics in the sun while watching the boaters work their way through the rapids.

If you aren't a boater, you can enjoy the river from the 2.5-mile trail that follows the St. Francis River from Silver Mines to Millstream Gardens. Along the way you'll hike through quiet forests, along high bluffs with great views, and next to the sometimes peaceful, sometimes violent St. Francis River. The hike starts at the boater's access on the north side of the river near the old MO D bridge and goes upstream. A half mile upriver is the old dam and mill site built during the area's mining days to power mining equipment. This relic is worth a look, and if the water is low you can cross the dam and hike back to camp on the south side of the river for a 1-mile loop. Along the way back to the campground you'll pass by an old mine shaft

---

To get there: From Fredericktown, drive 6.5 miles west on MO 72 to MO D, where you'll see a sign to Silver Mines Recreation Area. Turn left (south) on MO D and follow it 3 miles to Silver Mines. Summit, Prospect, and Spring Branch Loops are on the north side of the St. Francis River. Riverside Loop is on the south side of the river.

To reach Millstream Gardens, the west end of the trail and incredibly scenic site of the Missouri Whitewater Championships, drive 8 miles west of Fredericktown of MO 72, turn south at the wooden sign for Millstream Gardens, and follow a gravel road a half mile to the parking area.

KEY INFORMATION

Silver Mines Recreation Area
Mark Twain National Forest
P.O. Box 188
Potosi, MO 63664

Operated By: U.S. Forest Service

Information: (573) 438-5427

Open: March 15–October 30

Individual sites: 66 single sites, 9 double sites, 1 group campsite

Each site has: Picnic table, fire pit with grate, lantern pole

Site assignment: First come, first served; reservations available through National Recreation Reservation System (877) 444-6777 or ReserveUSA.com

Registration: Self-pay station at loop entrances

Facilities: Vault toilets, water spigots in each loop, picnic areas, canoe and kayak access

Parking: At individual site

Fee: $8 for single site, $16 for double site, $8.65 fee for reservation (nonrefundable); $2 day-use fee per vehicle for picnic area, swimming hole, and boater access parking lots; half-price with Golden Age Passport

Elevation: 600 feet

Restrictions:

Pets—Allowed on leash

Fires—In fire pits

Alcoholic beverages—Allowed, subject to local ordinances

Vehicles—Up to 30 feet

Other—14-day stay limit

called Air Conditioner. Complete with a small shed and benches for relaxing, it's a perfect break on a hot summer hike. Be careful crossing the dam, and don't even attempt it if the river is flowing strongly. If you're uncomfortable with crossing the dam, retrace your steps and hike up to the Air Conditioner and the dam from Riverside Loop.

Continuing upstream on the trail that follows the north riverbank, you'll pass Turkey Creek Picnic Area and then hike forests and hills for a mile and a half, until you reach Cat's Paw Rapid, where a viewing platform treats you to spectacular views up and down the St. Francis. Just beyond Cat's Paw, the river roars through the Tiemann Shut-Ins at Millstream Gardens, where you'll thump across an old covered bridge near the picnic area at the trail's end. Though the campground is closed in winter, I love to hike this trail when it's below freezing. The bitter cold grows spectacular ice formations in the river's rapids, and once I saw an eagle perched on a limb high above the St. Francis.

On the left side of MO D about a half mile west of Silver Mines, a quarter-mile trail winds through the ghost town of Silver Mountain. Built by Einstein Mining Company in the late 1800s, this town was once home to 800 souls. In its heyday it had a school, post office, and several stores. On the trail you can wander through the leftover foundations and sidewalks of this once-lively community.

Not the active type? Then head for the swimming hole, where you can alternate between cooling in the stream and sunbathing on the boulders that dot the riverbed. Or break out your fishing pole and drowse along the bank while you go after bass and bluegill. There's something for everyone at Silver Mines Recreation Area.

SUTTON BLUFF

Centerville, MO

Sutton Bluff Recreation Area is named for R.G. Sutton, who settled this valley on the Black River in 1888. Three generations of Suttons farmed the river bottoms below the impressive bluff just upstream from the campground. A pretty meander of the Black River curls around the campsites, and another wooded bluff rises steeply to the west to shade the campground in the late afternoon. Sutton Bluff is a wonderful place for hiking, picnicking, mountain biking, canoeing, swimming, or just hanging out.

The campsites at Sutton Bluff are scattered throughout a parklike grassy area with just enough trees to shade many of the sites. All camping spots here are good ones, but the best sites are at the beginning of the loop. Many of these are against the trees next to the Black River, with lots of shade and lush lawn surrounding them. Site 14 is the best of all—the most private spot in the campground. Sites closest to the river have two tables. Campsites 15–35 are on the gentle hillside sloping upward from the river. Most have level spots for tents, and those at the far end of the camp are quiet sites with a view of the rest of the campground. Water and toilets are scattered conveniently throughout the campground.

The river attracts many campers. You can fish right from the campground, hiking up or down stream to try your luck. The river-bend that wraps around the campground

CAMPGROUND RATINGS

Beauty:	★★★★★
Site privacy:	★★★
Site spaciousness:	★★★★
Quiet:	★★★
Security:	★★★★
Cleanliness/upkeep:	★★★★★

Hike the Sutton Bluff Trail for scenic views over a horseshoe bend in the Black River.

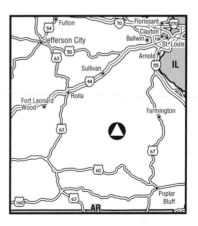

MARK TWAIN NATIONAL FOREST

is only a few steps away, and it's a great place to swim, wade, or relax in the sun with your lawn chair and a cold drink. Just upstream from camp, FS 2236 crosses the river on a slab bridge. The broad gravel bar above the bridge, overlooked by Sutton Bluff, is a wonderful place to play in the water or watch the sunset. The Black River is great for tubing, and canoe outfitters in nearby Lesterville can outfit you for a relaxing float through the forested mountains.

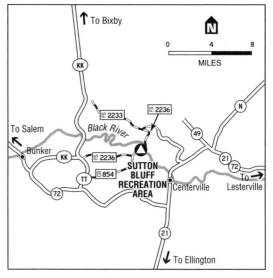

There are two places to mountain bike right from camp. One of these is the Sutton Bluff ATV Trails, a series of point-to-point routes of various lengths. Using forest roads as connectors, on the trail system you can ride loops of 3 to 10 miles. They're scattered along FS 2233 and are marked with orange posts and numbers. The campground host usually has maps of the Sutton Bluff ATV Trails, or you can contact the forest service in Salem.

The other bike ride follows the Karkaghne Section of the Ozark Trail. I always wondered where this strange name came from, and the folks at the Mark Twain National Forest finally gave me the straight scoop. Karkaghne is named for a mystical, dragon-like forest creature who usually walks backwards—it doesn't much care where it's going, but it likes to know where it's been. Only a few lucky individuals have seen this shy, secretive beast, usually through the bottom of a fruit jar recently emptied of moonshine. Well, that's what they told me.

Anyway, the Karkaghne Trail is tough but nice. It runs 18 miles west of Sutton Bluff to the junction of MO 72 and MO P. The first part is very rugged and has several long climbs, but once past mile 6 it's a good ride all the way to the trailhead at MO 72. You can make a 30-mile loop by biking the trail to MO 72, then returning to Sutton Bluff via MO 72, MO TT, CR 854, and FS 2236. The Karkaghne Trail leaves Sutton Bluff from the far end of the concrete bridge, heading uphill to the west.

The most scenic part of the Karkaghne Section of the Ozark Trail is right next to the camp. You can hike this beautiful path on the 2-mile Sutton Bluff Trail. Following the Karkaghne for its first mile, the loop switchbacks steeply up the northern end of the bluff overlooking the camp. Once near the top, it cuts straight across the cliff face, with beautiful overlooks and drop-offs steep enough to require handrails. Along the highest part of the hike you'll enjoy dramatic views of the Black River's horseshoe bend around the campground. Soon after the path leaves the scenic cliff-edge you'll come to a fork. The Sutton Bluff Trail follows the left fork, descends to the Black River, and follows the riverbank back to the trailhead.

While you're at Sutton Bluff, keep an eye peeled for those Karkaghnes. Since fruit jars aren't allowed in the river, you probably won't see any.

To get there: From Centerville, drive north 3 miles on MO 21 to Forest Road 2233, where a sign directs you to Sutton Bluff. Turn left and go 7 miles to FS 2236/County Road 849, where another sign directs you left 3 miles to the campground.

KEY INFORMATION

Sutton Bluff Recreation Area
Mark Twain National Forest
1301 S. Main Street
Salem, MO 65560

Operated by: U.S. Forest Service

Information: (573) 729-6656

Open: April 21–October 30

Individual sites: 33 single, 2 double

Each site has: Table, fire pit with grate, lantern pole; sites along the river have two tables

Site assignment: First come, first served; reservations available through National Recreation Reservation Service (877) 444-6777 or ReserveUSA.com

Registration: Self-pay at campground entrance

Facilities: Water, flush and vault toilets, picnic area, pavilion, trails, horseshoe pits

Parking: At individual site

Fee: $8 single site, $16 double, $2 per vehicle at picnic area, $25 pavilion; $8.65 fee for reservation (nonrefundable)

Elevation: 820 feet

Restrictions:

Pets—Allowed on leash

Fires—In fire pits

Alcoholic beverages—Allowed, subject to local ordinances

Vehicles—Up to 25 feet

Other—14-day stay limit; no glass containers in river

WATERCRESS SPRING

Van Buren, MO

Have you ever dreamed of slurping a chocolate shake while you were camping out under the open skies? Well, you can do just that at Watercress Spring Recreation Area. It feels like it's in the middle of nowhere, yet it's less than a mile from downtown Van Buren. It's a short walk to the Jolly Cone, where you can founder yourself on ice cream and then head back to your pretty campsite to complain about how much you ate.

Watercress Spring Recreation Area is next to the Current River, on a small flatland between the stream and the hills that separate the campground from Van Buren. Sites 1–10 are in a loop breaking off from the park road across from the picnic area. They are pretty sites under a medium-size bluff, with a spring branch flowing between the loop and the hillside. These campsites are shady and level but a little crowded together. Site 4, closest to the bluff and the stream, is the pick site in this loop.

Sites 11–17 are in a second loop, at the end of the park road. They are a little farther apart, and brush screens each site from its neighbors. Site 17, closest to the river, is a pretty camping spot. Across the road is site 11, another beautiful place to pitch your tent. It backs up to an open grassy meadow, perfect for a small group with several tents. Watercress Spring, with its gentle boils kicking up tiny volcanoes of sand, is at the far end of the meadow.

CAMPGROUND RATINGS

Beauty: ★★★★
Site privacy: ★★★
Site spaciousness: ★★★
Quiet: ★★★★
Security: ★★★★
Cleanliness/upkeep: ★★★★★

Where else in the Ozarks can you relax in a seemingly far-away-from-it-all riverside campground and be only a 1-mile walk from an ice cream stand?

MARK TWAIN NATIONAL FOREST

The Current River is the immediate attraction at this campground. It's wide and slow as it passes Watercress Spring, an ideal spot for tubing, swimming, wading, and fishing from the riverbanks. At one time this broad, shallow reach of the Current was used as a ford. During the Civil War, 3,000 Union troops camped here, with a mission of suppressing guerilla warfare in the surrounding countryside. They built breastworks on the hills above the current campground site and kept a close eye on the river crossing for Confederate operations.

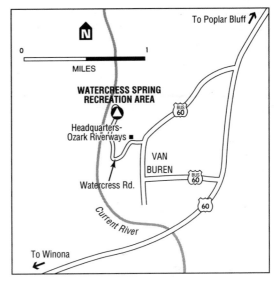

You can examine all that remains of their encampment from the 1.2-mile Songbird Trail. Beginning at the spring, this hike follows the spring branch and then climbs on to the hill above camp. From the ridge near the headquarters building you'll see the soldiers' old trenches on the slope below the trail. A plaque tells the legend of an old cannon that had to be left behind when the troops moved out. To keep it out of Confederate hands, the Union troops supposedly shoved it off the hillside into the spring branch flowing through camp. If the myth is true, the cannon is still buried in the silt under the calm spring creek at Watercress.

My favorite attraction in the area is the Ozark National Scenic Riverways' Big Spring, located 5 miles south of Watercress on MO 103. You can camp there, but for me it's too busy—a monstrous open campground with little shade, hundreds of sites, and little privacy. I'll use their coin-operated shower if I feel a little grubby, but I prefer camping at the more laid-back Watercress Spring and driving over to Big Spring to admire that area's beauty as a day-user.

Big Spring truly lives up to its name—it's the biggest spring in Missouri. Flowing 275 million gallons per day, it's a beautiful aquamarine wonder. Dye tracings show that this huge gusher draws water from a 1,000-square-mile area, pulling runoff from as far away as 50 miles. After admiring the spring, you can explore the area on the Chubb Hollow Trail and the Slough Trail. These short hikes take you through the bottoms along the spring branch, past the confluence of the branch and the Current River, and over the wooded ridges above Big Spring.

The architecture of the park's lodge and cabins is worth checking out. CCC Companies 734, 1710, and 1740 built them in the 1930s as part of what was then Big Spring State Park. The National Park Service has restored these beautiful old structures. The rustic lodge, built next to the confluence of Big Spring's outflow branch and the Current River, is a wonderful place to enjoy a relaxing meal while you admire the streams flowing together outside your window.

You can rent a canoe in Van Buren to float the Current. It's a 5-mile paddle from Watercress down to Big Spring, leaving you plenty of time to explore the area after drifting down from Watercress.

To get there: From Van Buren's town center, go east on US 60 Business to Watercress Road. There you'll see a sign directing you to the Ozark National Scenic Riverways Headquarters and Visitor Center. Turn north, drive a quarter mile to the visitor center, and on your left across from the visitor center you'll see the entrance to Watercress Recreation Area. Follow the blacktop road down the hill to the campground.

KEY INFORMATION

Watercress Spring Recreation Area
Mark Twain National Forest
Route 1, Box 1908
Winona, MO 65588

Operated by: U.S. Forest Service

Information: (573) 325-4233

Open: Year-round

Individual sites: 14 single, 3 double

Each site has: Table, fire pit with grate, lantern pole

Site assignment: First come, first served

Registration: Self-pay station at loop entrance

Facilities: Water, flush and vault toilets, pavilion, picnic area, trail, river access; water and flush toilets unavailable November 1–May 1

Parking: At individual site

Fee: $8 single site, $16 double, $25 for picnic pavilion

Elevation: 460 feet

Restrictions:

Pets—Allowed on leash

Fires—In fire pit

Alcoholic beverages—Allowed, subject to local ordinances

Vehicles—Up to 35 feet

Other—14-day stay limit, no glass containers in river or on its banks

BUFFALO
NATIONAL
RIVER

KYLES LANDING

Jasper, AR

Kyles Landing is my favorite camp-ground on the Buffalo National River. A low bluff overlooks Kyles, and a large pine grove in the downstream end of camp reminds me of the Rockies. The campground's rough, steep 3-mile entrance road keeps RVs and monster trailers away. Level grassy areas make it seem like you're camping in your back yard rather than in incredibly rugged and scenic parklands. The trails leading from Kyles are perfect avenues for exploring those towering hills and deep hollows.

As you enter Kyles and intersect the campground's loop road, the pine grove is on your right. Sites 1–10, scattered among these trees, are the best-shaded spots. Sites 5 and 6 are the most private, tucked far back in the evergreens. The loop then curves past the river access and sites 11–16 on an open lawn next to the river. Sites 17–19, nestled in a little meadow in the woods next to the Buffalo, are great camping spots. They offer good shade, privacy, and a swimming hole a few feet away. Sites 20–24 are spacious and in the center of the campground loop but have little shade and are near the bathrooms and their all-night lights. The remaining sites are against the woods at the edge of the campground. All sites are walk-in.

Avoid Kyles on spring weekends, especially Memorial Day and Easter, when floatable river levels attract hundreds of

CAMPGROUND RATINGS

Beauty: ★★★★★

Site privacy: ★★★

Site spaciousness: ★★★★★

Quiet: ★★★★

Security: ★★★★

Cleanliness/upkeep: ★★★★★

To see the best of the Buffalo, float the river 10 miles from Ponca to Kyles, spend a night next to the river, and spend the next day hiking the Ponca Wilderness.

BUFFALO NATIONAL RIVER

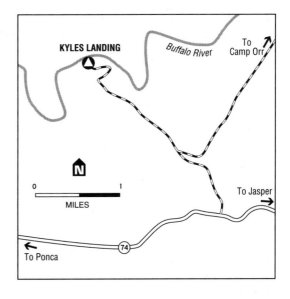

canoeists to the upper river. By mid-summer the hordes move downriver, and Kyles becomes a peaceful place. Fall attracts quite a few hikers, but they aren't as many or as rowdy as the spring canoeing parties. I like winter at Kyles—days are often sunny and warm, low river levels make easy river fords on hikes from the campground, and winter's lack of foliage opens up wonderful vistas along the river.

The trailhead lies at the campground's western end. You can choose between the Old River Trail that stays low along the river, the Buffalo River Trail that explores the highlands to the river's south, or the fantastic scramble up Indian Creek. When the river is waist-deep or less, I like the Old River Trail, a level 2 miles and four river crossings from Kyles west to Horseshoe Bend. The trail passes two old homesteads on the way, including one with an intact barn near a lonesome old stone chimney in the overgrowth. Horseshoe Bend has a wide rock bench above the river that's a great place for a picnic, backpack camping, or hanging out.

From Horseshoe Bend it's a 1-mile hike across the river north to Hemmed-In Hollow. Hemmed-In is a monstrous box canyon with a 175-foot waterfall pouring off the bluff and showering the canyon floor below. This place is spectacular in spring or after rain, when the falls are running wild. On your return, go right at the fork you passed on the way in. Follow it a half mile uphill to a trail junction. A quarter-mile hike uphill to the right leads to California Point and a vista of Hemmed-In Hollow. Check out the view, then take the left trail. It follows a benchland with great views of the river, then drops back to river level at Sneeds Creek, where you'll hit the Old River Trail. Just to your left will be the ruins of the Center Point School— I'd have loved to go to school there!

Horseshoe Bend and the route back to Kyles is a quarter mile to the left on the Old River Trail. For more spectacular scenery, go right instead, following signs to the Center Point Trailhead. A half mile from Sneed Creek is Granny Henderson's Cabin, an old farmhouse with a wonderful view from the front porch. From Granny's follow the Center Point Trail a mile uphill to another trail going left. This is the Goat Trail onto Big Bluff. It'll take you onto a narrow ledge 350 feet above the river for the best view in all of Arkansas. Be very careful out there—it's a long fall to the river. From Big Bluff it's 4 miles back to Kyles.

While you're at Kyles, don't miss Indian Creek, a primitive unmarked route breaking south off the Buffalo River Trail just west of camp. It's wonderful in spring or after rainstorms—water brings this hidden canyon to life. The trail is an unbelievable succession of waterfalls, pools, cascades, bluffs, and boulders. It features a cave with a waterfall gurgling from its mouth, with another cascade rushing down a 50-foot bluff behind it. If you climb the steep hillside opposite the cave, ease through a natural tunnel in the rock, and hike another quarter mile up-canyon to see a natural bridge called Eye of the Needle. Plan to spend all day in this magical canyon.

To get there: Take AR 74 5 miles west from Jasper or 10 miles east from Ponca. Turn north and follow a steep, crooked, and rough gravel road 3 miles to the campground.

KEY INFORMATION

Kyles Landing
Buffalo National River
402 N. Walnut, Suite 136
Harrison, AR 72601

Operated by: National Park Service

Information: (870) 741-5443, (870) 741-2884 TDD

Open: Year-round

Individual sites: 33

Each site has: Table, fire pit with grate, lantern pole

Site assignment: First come, first served

Registration: None required

Facilities: Water, flush and vault toilets, trails, river access; water turned off November–March

Parking: At lots near sites

Fee: No fee

Elevation: 900 feet

Restrictions:

Pets—Allowed on leash at campground; not allowed on trails

Fires—In fire pit

Alcoholic beverages—Allowed; limited to either 1 gallon wine, 1 gallon hard liquor, or 1 case of beer per vehicle; local ordinances apply

Vehicles—No length limit; RVs and trailers not recommended on steep and rough entrance road

Other—14-day stay limit; maximum 6 people per site; no glass containers in the river, in caves, on trails, or within 50 feet of any stream

LOST VALLEY

Boxley, AR

Like most of the Buffalo River country, Lost Valley and the landscape around it are magical places. The campground itself is only average, but the beauty you can discover on foot from the campground is incredible. Clark Creek drains the gorge above camp and rushes past your campsite on its way to the Buffalo River a mile downstream. The most popular trail in the Buffalo National River starts in the campground and follows the creek upstream. More trails, natural wonders, and historic attractions are only a few miles away.

Officially, all sites in Lost Valley are walk-in, but you can park next to sites 1 and 2, near the entrance, and at site 15 at the north end of the parking lot. The remaining sites are on the far side of Clark Creek from the parking lot. If the creek is low, a short walk directly across the streambed leads to sites 3–14. When the creek's deep, a longer walk to the footbridge at the north end of the camp offers dry access to all sites. Site 14 next to the footbridge is level and spacious, but my favorite is site 13. It's at the north end of the campground with lots of space and privacy. The remaining sites are good, but some are a little rocky, others a bit close together, and some aren't very level. All campsites are well shaded.

The campground usually fills on spring weekends when the river is floatable, but that's the best time to hike the Lost Valley Trail. It's a beautiful hike even when dry, but

CAMPGROUND RATINGS

Beauty:	★★★★★
Site privacy:	★★★
Site spaciousness:	★★★
Quiet:	★★★★
Security:	★★★★
Cleanliness/upkeep:	★★★★★

The Lost Valley Trail, which heads north from the campground, has more natural wonders per mile than any other trail in the Buffalo National River.

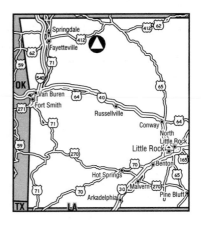

BUFFALO NATIONAL RIVER

water in the creek really brings the place alive. To avoid crowds, I wait for an off-season rain and then come here to camp and hike. This point-to-point trail with a short midpoint loop is a 3.5-mile round-trip through an enchanting canyon of natural wonders. At the first fork in the trail you see the first marvel—the Siamese Beeches, two huge trees that have grown together. Take the right fork and check out the Jig Saw Blocks, huge chunks of stone with contours matching the wall from which the stones fell.

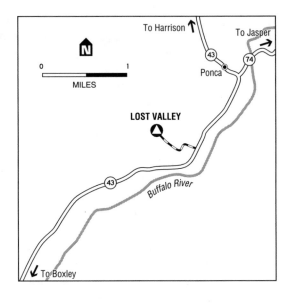

Just beyond the Blocks, Clark Creek flows through a 50-foot natural bridge. It's amazing to see the stream pour through a huge limestone wall and cascade down several ledges into a calm pool. Continuing down the trail, the next feature is Cob Cave, named for the corn cobs left there by prehistoric tribes that once lived in this hideaway. Cob Cave is a huge undercut in a 200-foot bluff, forming the perfect shelter for stormy weather.

Up-canyon from the cave is my favorite feature in Lost Valley—Eden Falls tumbling 170 feet down the head of the canyon. Admire it a bit from below and then take the trail up to near its top, where you'll find Eden Cave. Much of the flow for the Eden Falls gurgles out of this opening in the bluff. Bring a flashlight—if you crawl into the cave, you're in for a treat. The cave quickly narrows down to a wide, low crawl space, where a short scramble on all fours leads to a 40-foot tall chamber with a waterfall pouring from the ceiling. If you're not claustrophobic, it's worth crawling a few feet through solid rock to check out this otherworldly place!

Another spectacular sight near Lost Valley is Whitaker Point, better known as Hawksbill Crag, in the Upper Buffalo Wilderness. Photos of the crag have been on the cover of National Geographic, in outdoor product advertisements, and in lots of Arkansas Tourism literature. To get there from Lost Valley, take AR 43 west to AR 21, then go south 2 miles to the Buffalo River Bridge. Turn right on Cave Mountain Road, an unmarked gravel road just before the bridge. It climbs steeply up onto Cave Mountain and follows a ridge 6 miles to a trailhead on the right. It's a 1.5-mile hike to Hawksbill Crag, a huge cliff with a rock overhang above the Upper Buffalo Wilderness. You can walk right out onto the crag and be awed by the view over the upper reaches of the Buffalo River spread out below.

A half mile up Cave Mountain Road from AR 21, you passed Cave Mountain Cave. Early residents of the Boxley Valley used this large cavern for dances, weddings, revivals, and town meetings. During the Civil War, the Confederacy mined the cave's bat guano for saltpeter, an important ingredient for manufacturing gunpowder. In 1862 Union forces captured the installation and destroyed the equipment at the site. The huge kettles used in the operation were picked up by locals and used for livestock troughs, planters, and downspout barrels. On your way back to Lost Valley, you can see one of the kettles in a farmer's corral on the south side of AR 43. It looks like a huge upside-down army helmet.

To get there: From Ponca on AR 43 drive 2 miles southwest to a sign for Lost Valley. Turn north and drive a half mile north on a gravel road to the campground.

KEY INFORMATION

Lost Valley
Buffalo National River
402 N. Walnut, Suite 136
Harrison, AR 72601

Operated by: National Park Service

Information: (870) 741-5443, (870) 741-2884 TDD

Open: Year-round

Individual sites: 15 sites total, 3 park-in, 12 walk-in; sites 14 and 15 disabled accessible

Each site has: Table, lantern pole, fire pit with grate; sites 14 and 15 have barbecue grills on poles

Site assignment: First come, first served

Registration: None required

Facilities: Flush toilets, water, trail, amphitheater; water turned off November–March

Parking: In lot next to campground

Fee: Free

Elevation: 1,100 feet

Restrictions:

Pets—On leash in campground; not allowed on trails

Fires—In fire pits

Alcoholic beverages—Allowed but limited; local ordinances apply

Vehicles—No length limit, but no sites for RVs or trailers

Other—14-day stay limit; maximum 6 people per site; no glass containers in river, on trails, in caves, or within 50 feet of streams

O Z A R K

Jasper, AR

Ozark Campground has neither the grand bluffs of Steel Creek nor the hidden scenic wonders of Lost Valley, but this peaceful riverside hideaway is a comfortable place to relax. Its campsites form a ring around a grassy meadow next to the Buffalo River. The campground has both open and shaded campsites, access to good day floats upstream and downstream, and a pavilion for escaping hot sunshine or chilly rainstorms.

All these walk-in sites are level and spacious. Sites 1–6 are shaded, but they're close to the loop road and far from the river. Sites 7–14 are on a bench below the level of the rest of the campground. They're farthest from the road, requiring the longest walk. Sites 15–20, nestled against the fringe of trees next to the Buffalo, are closest to the river and not far from their parking spots. Sites 21–30 are shaded by a nice grove of trees, but since they are close to the entrance road they are sometimes dusted by incoming traffic. They don't have the nice grass of the other campsites but still are comfortable shady sites, only a few steps from the Buffalo.

Ozark is an excellent canoe camp. It's a 9-mile float downstream from Hasty, easily done in a day. Upstream, you can take a nice 12-mile float from Kyles Landing or a shorter 6-mile paddle from Erbie back to Ozark, drifting beneath impressive bluffs that tower above the river.

CAMPGROUND RATINGS

Beauty: ★★★★
Site privacy: ★★★
Site spaciousness: ★★★★
Quiet: ★★★★
Security: ★★★★
Cleanliness/upkeep: ★★★★★

With both shaded and sunny campsites, Ozark has good sites for both summer and winter adventures.

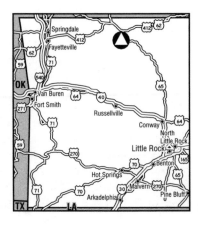

BUFFALO NATIONAL RIVER

The Buffalo River Trail passes Ozark, giving you hiking options right from your campsite. A 2.5-mile hike east takes you to Pruitt, the eastern terminus to this section of the trail. A 1.7-mile hike upstream goes to Cedar Grove Overlook, where there's a nice view of the river and a spur trail leads to a picnic area and two small, clear ponds. While you're hiking keep a sharp eye for elk—they're common in this part of the Buffalo National River.

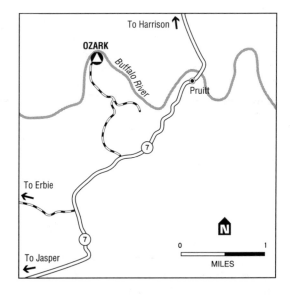

For more great hiking, go to Erbie, 1 mile south of Ozark on AR 7 and then 6 miles northwest on a gravel county road. There's a campground at Erbie, but it's not as nice as Ozark. It has little shade, the area around it gets a little overgrown, but it's a nice place to camp when Ozark is full. I like camping in Erbie's open environs during cooler times of the year when I want sunshine on my campsite. I also like Erbie for the nice hiking and the historical sites in that part of the river.

On your way to the Erbie Church trailhead you'll pass by a couple of these historical sites. Just past the campground is the Parker-Hickman farm, the oldest historic buildings in the park. Built in the 1840s and occupied until 1977, the farm consists of a house, two barns, a chicken coop, and several other outbuildings. You can walk through the site, check out the buildings, and imagine old days on the Buffalo.

You can hike right from the homestead, but the best trailhead is at another historic site—the Erbie Church, built in 1896 and still being used today. To reach it, continue northwest from the Parker-Hickman site, splash through the river on a slab bridge, and drive a half mile to a trailhead just past the old church. Before your hike, you can check out this peaceful house of worship.

Several trails take off from this trailhead, but my favorite is Cecil Cove Loop. It uses parts of the Cecil Cove Trail and the Farmer Trail for a 7.5-mile hike. Along Cecil Creek you'll see a spring and an impressive wall of rocks cleared from long-disappeared farm fields. You'll cross the creek several times and pass by the mouth of Beauty Cave, the longest cave in Arkansas.

The loop's southern half climbs to a ridge above Cecil Creek and passes several abandoned homesites and the haunting Jones Cemetery. Several tombstones for day-old infants will make you realize how tough times were in the early 20th century. Near the end of the loop you'll pass the J.W. Farmer homestead with its old house, two barns, and several outbuildings. The last leg of the hike goes past scenic Goat Bluff and a pretty overlook of the Buffalo River. When you get back to the trailhead, the picnic table there is a wonderful place for a well-deserved posthike snack.

You'll find several other shorter trails in the Erbie Trail System, and a 20-mile mountain bike ride using a combination of paved, gravel, and four-wheel-drive roads can be started right from your camp at Ozark. It passes through the Erbie district and is suitable for riders of all skill levels.

To get there: From Jasper, drive 4.5 miles north on AR 7 to a gravel road with a sign directing you to Ozark. Turn left and follow the gravel road 1.5 miles to the campground.

KEY INFORMATION

Ozark Campground
Buffalo National River
402 N. Walnut, Suite 136
Harrison, AR 72601

Operated by: National Park Service

Information: (870) 741-5443, (870) 741-2884 TDD

Open: Year-round

Individual sites: 30

Each site has: Table, fire pit with grate, lantern pole

Site assignment: First come, first served

Registration: No registration required

Facilities: Water, flush toilets, pavilion, phone, river access, trails

Parking: In parking areas near sites

Fee: No fee

Elevation: 800 feet

Restrictions:

Pets—Allowed on leash at campground; not allowed on trails

Fires—In fire pits

Alcoholic beverages—Allowed; limited to either 1 gallon wine, 1 gallon hard liquor, or 1 case of beer per vehicle; local ordinances apply

Vehicles—No length limit

Other—14-day stay limit; maximum 6 people per site; no glass containers in the river, in caves, on trails, or within 50 feet of any stream

RUSH LANDING
Yellville, AR

This campground is near the ghost town of Rush, "the town that zinc built." Discovery of zinc in the 1880s turned this sleepy little farming valley into a noisy boomtown. At one time 17 mines were operating along Rush and Clabber creeks. When in 1886 a faulty assay hinted of silver deposits, a smelter was built for processing the ore. No silver was found, but the smelter still stands in the old Morning Star Mining Company's abandoned mill complex.

Activity in the Rush Mining District reached its peak during World War I, when zinc prices jumped. Around 5,000 people lived and worked along Rush Creek in a community stretching from the present-day ghost town all the way to the Buffalo River. The end of the district near the Buffalo was called New Town, while the northern end, where old buildings still remain, was the village of Rush. Besides residences and mines, the banks of Rush Creek once held hotels, stores, a livery stable, a post office, a doctor's office, and a school.

When World War I ended and the bottom fell out of the zinc market, most of the mines shut down. Rush dwindled, but somehow held on until the 1960s, when the post office and school were finally closed. The Morning Star Mining Company sold off their holdings at about the same time. Most of the buildings were taken down, leaving only the haunting structures, scattered foundations, and mine shafts to evoke memories of the

CAMPGROUND RATINGS

Beauty: ★★★★
Site privacy: ★★
Site spaciousness: ★★★★★
Quiet: ★★★★
Security: ★★★★
Cleanliness/upkeep: ★★★★★

You'll feel the haunting presence of old times on the Buffalo River while exploring the abandoned homes and mine sites at Rush Landing.

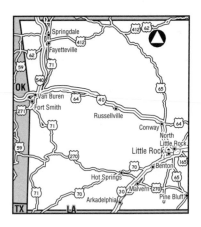

BUFFALO NATIONAL RIVER

wild times in Rush and New Town.

Where Rush Creek trickles into the Buffalo River, New Town once teemed with activity. Now you can camp the peaceful riverside where the village once stood. This campground is an appealing place to hang out. It has a river to swim, fish to catch, trails to hike, a ghost town to explore, and shade and sunshine to lay around in. The walk-in campground has camping areas that wrap around two sides of the parking area. Half the camp

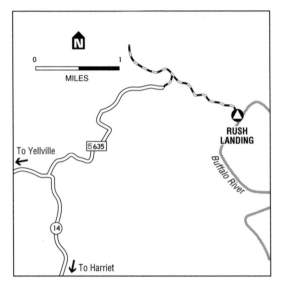

area is an open grassy meadow between the parking area and the river, with woods around the edge and a couple of trees here and there. The rest is a long, shady space stretching along Rush Creek. Nine tables and fire pits are scattered throughout the camping area. There are no specific sites—just find a spot you like and set up.

Across Rush Creek from the camp are the river access, picnic shelter, swimming hole, and trailhead. Spring, when most floaters are on the more-exciting upper Buffalo, is a nice time to come to Rush. Summer, when the upper river is no longer floatable and the crowds flock to the lower part of the Buffalo, is busiest. I love to come here in late fall and winter, when there's water in the river and nobody around except for the wandering ghosts of New Town and Rush.

Trailheads are at the river access near the campground and at the Morning Star mill site near the ghost town. The 1.6-mile Rush Mountain Trail connects the river access and the campground to the abandoned Morning Star Mining Company's mill complex. Along its way you'll pass lots of old mineshafts, tailings piles, and an abandoned mine car used for hauling ore out of the earth. From the river access, a spur off this trail leads to the old Monte Cristo mine and the Clabber Creek Overlook. From Monte Cristo there's an unofficial trail back to the Morning Star Trailhead, but it's rough and unmarked.

The Morning Star Trail is a 0.3-mile loop through the old Morning Star mill site. It passes the remains of the blacksmith shop, foundations of the old mill building, and the still-intact 1886 smelter. A sad stop on this loop is a photo and interpretive display of the Morning Star Barn. The barn stood intact on this site from the 1890s until December 1998, when it and the nearby Brantley house were burned to the ground by arsonists. A $1,000 reward has been offered for information leading to conviction of the vandals who destroyed these treasures.

A free guide for the Rush Mountain Trail is available at the Buffalo Point Information Station not far from Rush. While you're there, pick up a guide for the 3.5-mile Indian Rockhouse Trail at Buffalo Point and hike this wonderful interpretive trail. It showcases a bluff cave that once sheltered Native Americans and has many Ozark natural features. The Indian Rockhouse trailhead is near Buffalo Point's bluff-top restaurant, where you can enjoy some posthike snacking and admire the river valley hundreds of feet below your table.

To get there: Drive 11.5 miles southeast from Yellville on AR 14 to the marked road to Rush. Turn left and follow this paved and gravel road to a T intersection. Turn right and enter the Rush District. The camping area is 1.5 miles down on the right.

KEY INFORMATION

Rush Landing
Buffalo National River
402 N. Walnut, Suite 136
Harrison, AR 72601

Operated by: National Park Service

Information: (870) 741-5443, (870) 741-2884 TDD

Open: Year-round

Individual sites: Open, walk-in camping

Each site has: Open camping area has 9 tables with fire pits and grates

Site assignment: First come, first served

Registration: No registration required

Facilities: Vault toilets, river access, trails

Parking: In parking area next to campground

Fee: Free

Elevation: 475 feet

Restrictions:

Pets—Allowed on leash at campground; not allowed on trails

Fires—In fire pits

Alcoholic beverages—Allowed; limited to either 1 gallon wine, 1 gallon hard liquor, or 1 case of beer per vehicle; local ordinances apply

Vehicles—No length limit, but RVs and long trailers not recommended

Other—14-day stay limit; no glass containers on trails, in river, or within 50 feet of streams; do not enter abandoned mine shafts

STEEL CREEK

Ponca, AR

S teel Creek Campground is in a grassy bottomland tucked into a wide bend of the Buffalo River. Though its openness limits privacy, the place pays you back with wonderful views of this beautiful mile-long valley. Roark Bluff dominates the skyline to the north, overlooking the valley for most of its length. Heavy rains in Steel Creek are wonderful—downpours awaken the splendid waterfalls that cascade off Roark Bluff. One of the falls forms a curtain of whitewater rolling over the bluff edge. My favorite fall jets off the bluff across from camp and arches almost all the way across the river.

All sites at Steel Creek are walk-in, but because the campground is a long and narrow stretch of open grassland along the river, with parking along its entire length, it's not a long slog to any site. Take the extra effort to schlep your stuff to the far side of the campground, though—you'll get away from the dust of the gravel parking lot and will be in one of the 12 sites tucked into the riverbank trees, where there is shade and more privacy. The best spot is site 26 at the far end of the campground.

Steel Creek is very crowded in spring, when the upper river is in prime floating condition. If you like quiet, don't even consider coming here on Easter and Memorial Day weekends. Off-season is great—I once spent a rainy Thanksgiving weekend here, sharing the camp with a scattering of fellow campers and enjoying rare off-season

CAMPGROUND RATINGS

Beauty:	★★★★★
Site privacy:	★★
Site spaciousness:	★★★★★
Quiet:	★★★★
Security:	★★★★
Cleanliness/upkeep:	★★★★★

Steel Creek showcases the huge stone bluffs towering above the upper Buffalo River.

BUFFALO NATIONAL RIVER

floatable river levels. Once spring is past and the river levels drop, Steel Creek is a relaxing place to be. There's usually just enough water left in the river's pools for a cooling dip to offset summer heat, and the canoeing hordes are gone.

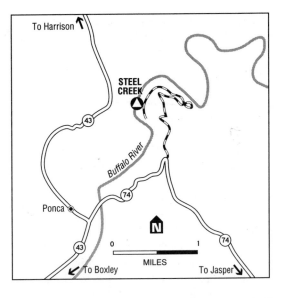

After canoeing, hiking is the prime activity at Steel Creek. Both Buffalo River and Old River Trails pass through the campground, giving you two upstream and two downstream hiking options. My favorite is the 2-mile hike on the Buffalo River Trail from Steel Creek to Ponca. It climbs out of camp up to Bee Bluff and follows its rim for a while. The bluff is named for a bee colony that lived high in the bluff for decades before settlers finally figured out how to get at the honey 80 feet above their heads. The trail passes a tall pillar leaning away from the bluff—close enough that you'll be tempted to jump out to it, but just far enough that you won't. Going farther on the trail will take you through a gap between the bluff and a slice that's broken away.

The last mile to Ponca is best. During and after rainstorms several waterfalls cascade down the hillside and splash into the Buffalo. At one point two waterfalls come snaking down the hillside, join forces near the trail, then continue downhill as a single roaring stream. At another cascade a quarter mile from Ponca, the stream rushes over a slickrock streambed for 100 feet, then plunges off a 50-foot bluff into the river. Just past this cascade is a stretch of trail on a bluff edge with nice views of the Buffalo.

The Buffalo River Trail east from camp is another great hike. In the first mile you'll walk over some tall rock ledges that sport a nice waterfall during wet times and pass a hollow tree big enough to squeeze inside. When you cross Steel Creek and start climbing, you'll be in the Ponca Wilderness—one of the most beautiful landscapes in Arkansas. A mile and a half from camp is the Steel Creek Overlook, one of the more scenic views in the park. On the outside of a sharp bend in the river, this cliff overlook surveys all the Steel Creek Valley, Roark Bluff upriver to the west, and a half-mile bluff extending downstream to the north.

Many hikers think the Old River Trail is just a horse path. I think it's a great hike all the way from Steel Creek to Kyles Landing. It follows the abandoned farm road that once served homesteads on the Buffalo, passing several ghostly tumbledown farms. Since it's an old road, the trail is level and easy most of the way. Lots of river crossings make this a fun hike on hot days. This is a great off-season hike when river levels are often so low that you won't even have to take your boots off at crossings.

The Old River Trail offers easy access to some of the coolest places in the Ponca Wilderness with very little hill work. From Steel Creek it's 4 miles to Horseshoe Bend, and 5 miles to Hemmed-In Hollow and Granny Henderson's Cabin. If you're energetic, another mile uphill from Granny Henderson's will get you to the spectacular Goat Trail on Big Bluff.

To get there: Drive 1 mile east from Ponca on AR 74. At the top of the long climb from Ponca, the entrance to Steel Creek will be on your left. Take this winding and steep gravel road 1 mile to Steel Creek.

KEY INFORMATION

Steel Creek
Buffalo National River
402 N. Walnut, Suite 136
Harrison, AR 72601

Operated by: National Park Service

Information: (870) 741-5443, (870) 741-2884 TDD

Open: Year-round

Individual sites: 26

Each site has: Table, lantern pole, fire pit with grate

Site assignment: First come, first served

Registration: None required

Facilities: Vault and flush toilets, trails, river access, water; water turned off November–March

Parking: Park in lot south of walk-in campsites

Fee: No fee

Elevation: 1,000 feet

Restrictions:

Pets—On leash at campground; not allowed on trails

Fires—In fire pits

Alcoholic beverages—Allowed; limited to either 1 gallon wine, 1 gallon hard liquor, or 1 case of beer per vehicle; local ordinances apply

Vehicles—No length limit; steep and winding entrance road not well-suited for RVs and long trailers

Other—14-day stay limit; maximum 6 people per site; no glass containers in river, on trails, in caves, or within 50 feet of streams

TYLER BEND

Silver Hill, AR

This picturesque campground is nestled into Tyler Bend of the Buffalo National River. Had the Army Corps of Engineers had its way, Tyler Bend would be under water. Just downstream is the site of a proposed 1960s dam site on the Buffalo. Plans to drown the Buffalo River country sparked conservation efforts that created this beautiful national park.

Tyler Bend's visitor center is a wonderful introduction to the Buffalo River Country. In addition to books, maps, and various exhibits, the center shows a movie covering the geology, wildlife, and history of the area. The film includes interviews with descendants of original settlers in the rugged country along the Buffalo. Their stories bring to life the haunting tumbledown homesteads scattered throughout the park.

The campground is in an open area that was once farm fields. Consequently, it does not yet have good shade in all sites, but the park service has planted many trees that provide better cover with each passing season. All sites are spacious, level, grassy, and nicely landscaped with picnic tables on stone pads. Sites 9, 12, 13, 19, and 22 have the best shade.

The walk-in campsites are spaced farther apart than the drive-in sites. Backed up against the trees fringing the river, they offer a little shade and have more privacy than the drive-in sites. A grassy expanse between the walk-ins and their parking area is a perfect

CAMPGROUND RATINGS

Beauty:	★★★★★
Site privacy:	★★
Site spaciousness:	★★★★★
Quiet:	★★★★
Security:	★★★★★
Cleanliness/upkeep:	★★★★★

For a perfect introduction to the Buffalo River Country, stop by the national park visitor center at Tyler Bend Campground.

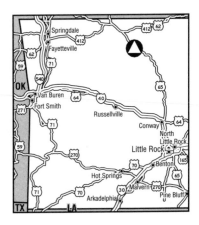

BUFFALO NATIONAL RIVER

place for sunbathing or tossing a Frisbee. I like the walk-in sites best, especially site J at the far south end of the campground.

Though the campground here is a bit overdeveloped, I included it because there is much to do in the area. For starters, canoeing above and below Tyler Bend is wonderful. Downstream from camp the Buffalo is usually floatable year-round. From Tyler Bend to the river village of Gilbert is an easy 5.6-mile float. On the way you'll drift around horseshoe-shaped Lane Bend, a 2.5-mile meander that you could cross on a quarter-mile hike. Gilbert itself is a quaint little town at the end of the road, with a general store stocked with items from today as well as antiques.

For a longer float, shuttle upstream to Woolum Ford and paddle 15 miles back to Tyler Bend. In spring, when the river flows faster, you can make this scenic trip in a day, coasting beneath majestic bluffs that tower over eight bends in the serpentine course of the Buffalo.

Six miles of trails await you at Tyler Bend. You can add miles by hiking the Buffalo River Trail east and west of the Tyler Bend trail system. Downstream, the Buffalo River Trail goes 6 miles to its current eastern terminus at Gilbert. Upstream, the Buffalo River Trail connects to the Ozark Highlands Trail at Woolum Ford, where you can hike almost 200 miles west to Lake Fort Smith. Trailheads are next to the amphitheater, next to the visitor center, and at the Collier Homestead a mile up the entrance road.

The prettiest hike at Tyler Bend is the River View Trail, a half-mile stretch on bluffs above the river, upstream from the campground. Depending upon which trailhead and connecting trails you choose, you can hike this path above the river on loops ranging in length from 1 to 4 miles. Besides passing spectacular views, the River View Trail loops also visit the nearly intact house at the Collier Homestead. Flowers still bloom in the yard so many springs after the Colliers left. When you see irises and daffodils blooming near an Ozarks trail, you're often near someone's abandoned home-site.

Bring your mountain bike to Tyler Bend—the 19-mile Snowball Loop takes you to one of the best views on the Buffalo. Suitable for beginners, this trail follows a combination of pavement, gravel roads, and four-wheel-drive paths to Peter Cave Bluff, where you'll admire a hairpin bend in the Buffalo 250 feet below your perch on the cliff. Just upstream on the hillside is a bare spot known as the Tie Slide. Timbers for railroad ties were once cut in the forest along the bluff, shoved down the steep hillside into the river below, and floated downstream to Gilbert.

Buffalo River Outfitters on US 65 at the park entrance has maps of the loop and rents mountain bikes. You can also reach Peter Cave Bluff and the Tie Slide by hiking the Buffalo River Trail 4 miles west from the Collier Homestead. Check at the visitor center or at Buffalo River Outfitters for maps and directions.

To get there: Head 30 miles southeast of Harrison on US 65. The Tyler Bend entrance is at Silver Hill. Turn west off US 65 and follow the paved road 3 miles to the campground.

KEY INFORMATION

Tyler Bend
Buffalo National River
402 N. Walnut, Suite 136
Harrison, AR 72601

Operated by: National Park Service

Information: (870) 439-2502, (870) 741-2884 TDD

Open: Year-round

Individual sites: 28 drive-in sites, 10 walk-in sites, 5 group sites

Each site has: Table, fire pit with grate, lantern pole

Site assignment: First come, first served; reservations available for group sites only

Registration: Self-pay at campground entrance

Facilities: Water, flush toilets, showers, dump station, amphitheater, pavilion, picnic area, visitor center, phone

Parking: At site for drive-in sites, in adjacent lots for group and walk-in sites

Fee: $10 individual site, $20 minimum group site

Elevation: 600 feet

Restrictions:

Pets—On leash at campground; not allowed on trails

Fires—In fire pits

Alcoholic beverages—Allowed but limited

Vehicles—Up to 40 feet

Other—14-day stay limit; no more than 6 people per individual site; no glass containers in river, within 50 feet of streams, on trails, or in caves

OZARK NATIONAL FOREST

BLANCHARD SPRINGS

Mountain View, AR

Blanchard Springs Recreation Area, hidden away deep in a narrow forested valley, is one of the most beautiful campgrounds in the Ozark Mountains. Though Blanchard Springs is a popular destination, the campground is at the far end of the complex where it's peaceful even on the busiest weekend. Sylamore Creek, a clear spring-fed creek, meanders through camp, paralleled by the Sylamore Creek Trail. There are two swimming holes in the creek, miles of trail to hike, and caverns to explore. Nearby Ozark Folk Center is a wonderful place to learn about Ozark Mountain history and traditions.

As you enter Blanchard Springs, you'll get a quick tour of the area, passing the caverns on the descent from AR 14. Turn left at the T at the bottom of the hill, drive past the picnic area and beach, and cross Sylamore Creek into the first campground. A spur to the right leads to sites 1–8, which are packed a little too close together. To the left are sites 9–13, with much better spacing between each camp. Sites 9, 11, and 14 are choice sites next to Sylamore Creek.

To reach the best campsites, drive past site 14, splash through the creek on a concrete slab, and pull into the upper campground loop with sites 16–31. This remote loop at the far end of the complex is very quiet, has secluded sites, and even has its own swimming hole near the loop entrance. Sites 16, 19, 20, and 21 are wonderful camping spots

CAMPGROUND RATINGS

Beauty:	★★★★★
Site privacy:	★★★★★
Site spaciousness:	★★★★
Quiet:	★★★★
Security:	★★★★
Cleanliness/upkeep:	★★★★★

Blanchard Springs Recreation Area's caverns, springs, swimming holes, and towering pines cool you on the hottest summer day.

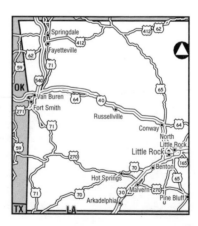

OZARK NATIONAL FOREST

on the banks of Sylamore Creek. Behind site 28 a spur trail leads to the Sylamore Creek Hiking Trail. Sites 26a and 26b form a double site for small groups and families. This back loop is definitely the place to be.

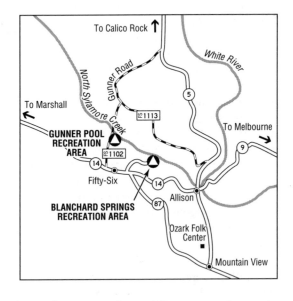

Blanchard Springs is a wonderful place to be during the heat and humidity of an Arkansas summer. Stately old pines and hardwoods shade all 32 sites. A beautiful swimming hole is just downstream from the campground, which is complete with a gravel beach, shower house, picnic sites, and impressive rock outcroppings. After your swim, go to the picnic area and check out Shelter Cave, a deep undercut hideout at the base of a tall bluff.

Another place to beat the heat is Blanchard Springs, at the opposite end of the recreation area from the campground. A paved trail with beautiful stonework bridges, walls, and steps leads out to a low bluff in the hillside where the spring tumbles from its outlet and splashes into a pool. Gushing 5,000 chilly gallons per minute, the spring water cools the hollow below the outlet before it's caught in Mirror Lake just downstream. The cold waters of the lake are home to a trout population just waiting for you to try your luck.

The coolest place in the park is Blanchard Springs Caverns, a living cave whose formations are still growing. The caverns showcase otherworldly stalactites, stalagmites, columns, walls of flowstone, and underground lakes and streams that feed the spring you just visited. The visitor center offers exhibits and a movie about the cave's development and geologic history, and guided tours are available to lead you through the caverns' wonders. The Dripstone

Trail Tour, an easy half-mile tour through a series of grand rooms full of cave formations, is offered year-round. The Discovery Trail Tour goes more deeply into the caverns. Covering 1.2 miles and more than 600 steps, this strenuous tour is well worth the effort. On the Discovery Trail you'll see underground lakes in the caverns' third level, check out the cave's natural entrance, and see uncounted fantastic crystalline formations. The Discovery Trail Tour is only offered in summer.

When you go back outside, take a hike on the 14-mile Sylamore Creek Trail. It begins near the White River 5 miles east of camp and runs to Barkshed Recreation Area 9 miles to the west, following the clear pools and riffles of North Sylamore Creek the entire way. A good destination is Gunner Pool Recreation Area, 5 trail miles west of Blanchard Springs. The last mile before Gunner Pool has impressive bluffs and vistas. Site of CCC Camp Hedges in the 1930s, Gunner Pool, with scenic cliffs overlooking North Sylamore Creek, must have been a great place to live and work. The rest of the Sylamore Creek Trail to Barkshed continues past more bluffs, creeks, and hollows just as beautiful as those you'll see on your way to Gunner Pool. Spend a few days at Blanchard Springs and hike this backcountry gem.

To get there: Drive 14 miles northwest of Mountain View on AR 14. The entrance to Blanchard Springs will be on the right. The visitor center and caverns are 1.5 miles down the road, and the campground and recreation area are another 1.5 miles past the visitor center.

KEY INFORMATION

Blanchard Springs Recreation Area
Ozark National Forest
P.O. Box 1279, Highway 14 N.
Mountain View, AR 72560

Operated by: U.S. Forest Service

Information: (870) 269-3228

Open: Year-round

Individual sites: 32 single, 2 group

Each site has: Table, fire pit with grate, lantern pole, grill

Site assignment: First come, first served

Registration: Self-pay at beginning of each loop

Facilities: Water, showers, flush toilets, swimming beach and bathhouse, amphitheater, picnic area, pavilions, visitor center, cave tours, trails

Parking: At individual site

Fee: $10 single site, $1.25 per person group site (minimum 8 people), $2 per vehicle in day-use areas

Elevation: 400 feet

Restrictions:

Pets—Allowed on leash; not allowed on beach

Fires—In fire pits

Alcoholic beverages—At campsite only

Vehicles—Up to 25 feet

Other—5-night stay limit in summer, 14-night stay limit rest of year; no more than 6 persons per site; no glass containers on beach or in creek; no jumping off rocks

COVE LAKE

Paris, AR

Cove Lake Recreation Area was built by the Civilian Conservation Corps and the Works Progress Administration during the Great Depression. The CCC's signature stonework is especially impressive in Cove Lake's bathhouse and picnic area. Rock terraces step down from the building to a grassy field beside the sandy beach on the lake. Wooded hills rise above the 160-acre lake on three sides, and Mt. Magazine, the tallest mountain in the Ozarks, overlooks the area from the south.

Cove Lake is especially beautiful in morning. Both times I've camped there, wisps and clouds of fog drifted above the lake, shining pink and gold in the sunrise. Many campsites are near the lakeshore, so you'll have nice vantage points to watch the same show while enjoying Ozark mornings at Cove Lake.

There are two sets of campsites in Cove Lake's campground. Loop A (sites 1–16) is open all year. All campsites are shady and level, with stone-lined tent pads that match the CCC stonework in the nearby day-use area. Several sites are terraced into the hillside below road level. Sites 11–16 are all beautiful lakeside camping spots. Site 10 isn't near the lake, but it's one of the most spacious sites in Loop A. Site 16 is my favorite site in this loop. It's private, has an excellent view of the lake, and sports a terraced tent pad and picnic table.

Loop B (sites 17–28) is closed during winter. Though it's farther from the day-use

CAMPGROUND RATINGS

Beauty:	★★★★★
Site privacy:	★★★★
Site spaciousness:	★★★★★
Quiet:	★★★★
Security:	★★★★
Cleanliness/upkeep:	★★★★★

Cove Lake is only a few miles from Mt. Magazine, the highest point in the Ozarks. Drive up the mountain and enjoy the vistas!

OZARK NATIONAL FOREST

area, it's still a great place to camp. Sites 17–24 overlook the water, and a small playground makes Loop B a good place for families. The pick camping spot in this loop is site 22. Located on its own little peninsula, it's by far the most private site at Cove Lake.

You can have fun at Cove Lake without leaving the campground. Campsites in this forested lakeside retreat are nice for reading, writing, napping, or simply shooting the breeze. There's a wonderful beach for swimming,

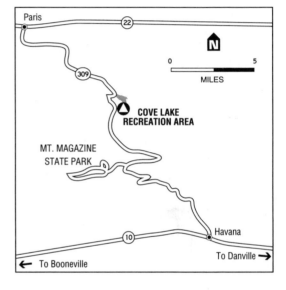

and snacks and cold drinks are available at a snack bar on summer weekends. You can rent a paddleboat or canoe to explore the lake. Fishing boats are available for going after Cove Lake's bass and sunfish populations. Luckily, a no-wake rule on holidays and weekends means motorboats on the lake won't take away from the peace and quiet in your campsite.

Bring your hiking boots to Cove Lake. Around the lake are 4.4 miles of the Cove Lake Trail, which takes you past the old Corley CCC camp. If you stick to the shortest option, you can take a 3-mile hike around the lake, finishing by crossing the dam on AR 309. A 1.1-mile side loop climbs the steep hillside north of the lake, and a 0.8-mile spur to the south climbs to the top of Flattop Mountain and a scenic overlook of Cove Lake and it surrounding mountains.

The best hike is the 14-mile Mt. Magazine Trail, stretching from Cove Lake to the peak of 2,753-foot Mt. Magazine. It's 11 miles to the peak, then 3 miles to the terminus at the East End or Greenfield picnic areas. Along the way you'll enjoy lots of scenic views, admire bluffs on the peak of Mt. Magazine, and experience intense satisfaction from climbing to the highest point in Arkansas.

Of course, you could shuttle to the top and hike down, but I like to hike uphill. That way I get a great workout and save the best scenery as a reward for reaching the top. The trail does have two road crossings that serve as bail-out points if you need them.

Whether you hike, drive, or bike, don't miss visiting Mt. Magazine and its scenic, breezy overlooks. The peak is especially nice in summer—temperatures are often 10 degrees cooler than the flatlands 2,000 feet below. If you're a climber, bring your gear. The bluffs around the mountain's relatively flat summit have dozens of challenging routes rated from 5.6 to 5.12c. Mountain breezes make those same bluffs a popular launch site for hang gliders. Bring your camera and binoculars and admire their effortless soaring on Mt. Magazine's updrafts.

For many years this beautiful mountaintop was a national forest recreation area. Now it's become part of the state park system. In 2000, construction of the Natural State's newest jewel was in full swing. Mt. Magazine State Park will have a Visitor Education Center, lodge, cabins, conference facilities, swimming pool, and campground. The paved roads are already in, and they have nice bike lanes for two-wheel exploration of the overlooks. Since the campground will be small and will offer full hookups, you'll probably still prefer to camp at Cove Lake. Then you'll have the best of both worlds—peaceful campsites at Cove Lake and a mountain to explore in your backyard.

To get there: From Paris, drive 9 miles southeast on AR 309. The campground is on the east side of the highway.

KEY INFORMATION

Cove Lake Recreation Area
Ozark National Forest
P.O. Box 511, 3001 E. Walnut
Paris, AR 72855

Operated by: U.S. Forest Service

Information: (501) 963-3076

Open: Year-round

Individual sites: 28

Each site has: Table, tent pad, fire pit with grate, lantern pole

Site assignment: First come, first served; reservations available through National Recreation Reservation Service (877) 444-6777 or ReserveUSA.com

Registration: Self-pay at campground entrance

Facilities: Water, flush and vault toilets, showers, picnic area, amphitheater, beach, sand volleyball, paddleboat and canoe rental, playground, trail; water turned off November 1–April 1

Parking: At individual site

Fee: $7 per site, $3 day-use fee per vehicle, $30 season pass for day-use area; $8.65 fee for reservation (nonrefundable)

Elevation: 1,040 feet

Restrictions:

Pets—Allowed on leash

Fires—In fire pits

Alcoholic beverages—At site only

Vehicles—Up to 35 feet

Other—14-day stay limit, no glass containers on beach

DEVIL'S DEN STATE PARK
West Fork, AR

D evil's Den, established in 1933, is one of Arkansas' oldest and most beautiful state parks. It covers 2,200 acres in the scenic Lee Creek Valley, with another 10,000 acres of the Ozark National Forest to the south and west. This rugged landscape awaits your exploration on the hiking and mountain biking trails lacing the forested hills.

The Civilian Conservation Corps built Devil's Den's facilities in the 1930s. These fascinating old buildings were renovated in 1970 and are some of the finest examples of CCC native stone and timber construction in the Ozarks. During their construction a CCC camp operated in the valley where the visitor facilities now stand. An interpretive trail takes you past the remains of the camp and tells the story of one of the many CCC companies that built such excellent recreation sites in the Ozarks.

Campsites are scattered throughout the Lee Creek Valley in seven separate areas. Loop A (sites 1–24) has the best tent camping. It's on a dead-end road far from the park's busier areas. The sites in Loop A are a little close together, but all are level, spacious, and shady. Some sites are next to Lee Creek, and others back up to a steep hill rising above the camp to the west.

Loop A is the access point for the eight walk-in sites at Devil's Den. From a parking area near the creek it's a level walk of several hundred yards along the Lee Creek Trail to the walk-ins. These are the most secluded

CAMPGROUND RATINGS

Beauty:	★★★★★
Site privacy:	★★
Site spaciousness:	★★★★
Quiet:	★★★★
Security:	★★★★
Cleanliness/upkeep:	★★★★★

Like many Arkansas recreation areas, Devil's Den State Park was built by the Civilian Conservation Corps. The park features an interpretive trail through the site of the CCC camp that once existed in this picturesque Ozark valley.

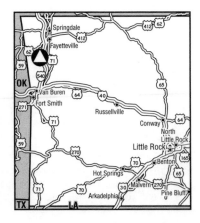

OZARK NATIONAL FOREST

sites at Devil's Den. Sites 1 and 2 are on the trail leading to a central clearing in the woods, where there's vault toilet. Sites 3–6 are on spurs leading away from the clearing. Sites 7 and 8 are on a dead-end spur at the far end of the walk-in campground. They're the most secluded sites in Devil's Den.

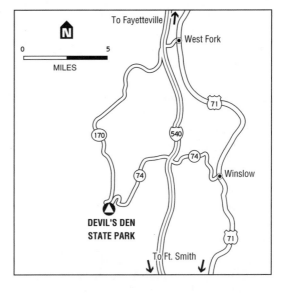

Sites 25–45 in loops B and C are too close to the park road and its traffic. Loop C is normally reserved for groups. Loop B's sites are best suited to RVs and trailers, as are sites 46–51 in loop D. Loop E (sites 52–97) is a very nice campground. All its sites have water and electricity, but the campground is quiet, shady, and many sites overlook the creek. Loop E also has a ball field, amphitheater, and a new bathhouse. Sites 101–143 are in the horse camp and are best suited to equestrians and their trailers. Stick to Loop A, the walk-ins, or Loop E, and you'll have a fine camping spot.

Devil's Den is perfect for exploration on foot. The 15-mile Butterfield Trail is popular for both backpackers and day hikers. It passes old homesteads, a washed-out CCC bridge, the abandoned community of Anna, and several scenic vistas. The Holt Ridge Overlook, a 0.6-mile side hike off the trail, is the most scenic view in the Lee Creek Valley. Several shorter trails offer additional hiking opportunities in Devil's Den.

Devil's Den is a mountain bike heaven. The park's administration embraced the sport from its inception in the early 1980s. The Ozark Mountain Bike Festival enlivens the park each spring, and the Ozark Mountain Bike Championships take place each September. Explore the park on the Fossil Flats Trail, an easy 3-mile loop that's perfect for beginners, or on the more challenging Holt Road Loop. Holt Road's 10-mile ride covers rocky terrain on single- and double-track paths. It follows the Butterfield Trail for a while, passing abandoned homesteads, a spring, and several scenic overlooks.

You can relax after your hike or bike ride at the park's swimming pool. Near the pool is a CCC dam on Lee Creek that forms an 8-acre lake, where you can rent paddleboats or canoes. Overlooking the lake is the Ridge Runner Cafe, where breakfast or lunch will hit the spot before you hit the trail.

Devil's Den has events and interpretive programs year-round. In addition to the mountain bike festivals and races, you'll find guided hikes, nature talks, recreation programs, and history walks through the old CCC camp.

A trip to the park's visitor center is a must. Besides exhibits on the park's natural and human history, the center has maps of the hiking, biking, and interpretive trails in the park. Permits are needed for overnight backpacking on the Butterfield Trail, and rangers ask that all mountain bikers check in with them before hitting the trail. Whether you're hiking or biking, they're ready to help you choose a route to match your abilities and interests and to tell you where all the cool stuff is at Devil's Den.

To get there: From Fayetteville, drive south on I-540 to West Fork Exit 53. Turn west on AR 170 and follow it 17 miles to the park. From Fort Smith, drive north on I-540 to Winslow Exit 45. Turn west on AR 74 and drive 7 miles to Devil's Den.

KEY INFORMATION

Devil's Den State Park
11333 W. AR Highway 74
West Fork, AR 72774
Operated by: AR State Parks
Information: (501) 761-3325
Open: Year-round
Individual sites: 97 drive-in sites, 8 walk-in sites, 43 horse-camp sites
Each site has: Table, fire pit with grate, lantern pole, tent pad
Site assignment: Sites assigned at visitor center; advance reservations available
Registration: Register at visitor center before occupying site
Facilities: Water, showers, flush toilets, laundry, phone, picnic area, pavilion, amphitheater, trails, visitor center, cabins, store, restaurant; during winter, water and showers available only in Loop B
Parking: At site; at special area for walk-ins
Fee: $5.50 walk-in site, $8.50 basic site, $11.50 electric site, $13.50 standard water and electric site, $15.50 preferred water and electric site
Elevation: 1,000 feet
Restrictions:
Pets—Allowed on leash
Fires—In fire pits
Alcoholic beverages—At site only
Vehicles—Up to 40 feet
Other—14-day stay limit; no glass containers on trails

GUNNER POOL

Fifty-Six, AR

The pleasant campground at Gunner Pool Recreation Area isn't just another of the excellent facilities built during the Great Depression by the Civilian Conservation Corps—it's the old site of an actual CCC camp. Over 2,200 young men went through what was then known as Camp Hedges, home of Company 743. A normal complement of 170 enrollees worked here, at this pretty streamside hideaway in the Ozarks.

Little remains of the old CCC camp, but when you settle in at Gunner Pool, you'll wish you could spend as much time here as the Civilian Conservation Corps did. North Sylamore Creek trickles through camp, overlooked by low bluffs next to the lower campground. Gunner Pool, namesake for this comfortable hideaway, is a small lake on a side stream of North Sylamore Creek. Though FS 2011 passes through the campground, there is little traffic to disrupt the calm at Gunner Pool. A fine grove of trees makes nearly every campsite a shady one.

Gunner Pool's campsites are divided into three areas. Sites 1–14 are on either side of a loop road on the east part of FS 2011 as you enter the recreation area. Most sites are adequately separated from their neighbors by good spacing and belts of trees. Sites 2 and 3 offer the best privacy on this loop. Sites 4 and 5 and sites 6 and 7 are paired campsites on spurs 100 feet off the main loop, with tent and table pads terraced into the hillside. While these paired sites are very close to

CAMPGROUND RATINGS

Beauty: ★★★★★

Site privacy: ★★★★

Site spaciousness: ★★★

Quiet: ★★★★

Security: ★★★★

Cleanliness/upkeep: ★★★★★

From Gunner Pool you can hike the North Sylamore Trail, mountain bike quiet forest roads, or wade in the cool waters of Sylamore Creek.

OZARK NATIONAL FOREST

each other, they are secluded from the other sites on the loop. They are perfect for small groups wishing to camp together. Sites 1, 9, 10, and 14 are spacious sites in the middle of the loop and are great camping spots for stargazers.

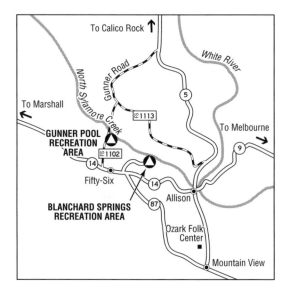

Across the road from sites 1–14 are three walk-in sites next to a small picnic area. Just north of the picnic sites is a second loop, containing sites 15–19. Site 16 is a pretty spot next to Gunner Pool's dam. Campsites 17 and 18 are roomy and located on the outside of this small loop. On the fringe of the campground, with views of the pool, they are the most private sites in the campground.

Sites 20–24 are the most popular camping spots at Gunner Pool. Located below the main campground on a spur road next to North Sylamore Creek, they are the prettiest spots in camp. A bluff towers over the creek and campsites. Site 21 is the pick site in the lower area. At the end of the road and close to the stream, it's shaded and private. Sites 22 and 23 are beautiful spots close to the stream, but other campers might pass through on their way to North Sylamore Creek.

Splashing in the creek is a fine way to while away the hours at Gunner Pool. So is relaxing in your campsite reading, writing, or shooting the breeze. This campground is popular in summer, often filling on weekends when school is out. It's also busy in October, when fall colors and festivals in nearby Mountain View attract travelers to the area.

I like Gunner Pool in winter or early spring, when I have it to myself. Those seasons are best for my favorite activity—hiking Ozark trails. The 14-mile North Sylamore Creek Trail passes right through Gunner Pool. A quarter-mile walk south of camp goes to a scenic overlook from the bluffs above the creek. Hiking 5 miles south, you'll pass several scenic spots on your way to Blanchard Springs—a beautiful day-use area and campground, where you can cool down on an underground tour of Blanchard Springs Caverns (see our profile on Blanchard Springs on page 106).

A 4-mile hike north from camp goes to Barkshed Recreation Area, a wonderful place to end a hike on a hot day. North Sylamore Creek has a pretty swimming hole below a small bluff at Barkshed. If you can't hike that far, drive or bike the wooded forest roads to Barkshed and check out this pretty hideaway. There's a campground at Barkshed, but it's not as nice as Gunner Pool.

While you're at Gunner Pool, drive 15 miles east to Mountain View and wander around Ozark Folk Center State Park. It showcases the heritage of the Ozark Mountain region with crafts demonstrations, music, cooking, and more. During tourist season (mid-April through early November) you can enjoy concerts and watch artisans demonstrate crafts like pottery, quilting, blacksmithing, and other skills needed to survive the old times in the Ozarks. To really get into the Ozarks culture, take one of the workshops on dulcimer, banjo, and autoharp. After class, come back to camp and practice by the fire until the wee hours. Quietly, of course.

To get there: From the town of Fifty-Six, turn north on AR 14 and follow FS 1102 3 miles to Gunner Pool. A sign just west of town marks the turn.

KEY INFORMATION

Gunner Pool Recreation Area Ozark National Forest P.O. Box 1279, Highway 14 N. Mountain View, AR 72560

Operated by: U.S. Forest Service

Information: (870) 269-3228

Open: Year-round

Individual sites: 27

Each site has: Table, fire pit with grate, lantern pole, tent pad; some sites have barbecue grill

Site assignment: First come, first served

Registration: Self-pay in center of upper campground

Facilities: Water, vault toilets, picnic area, trail; water turned off during winter

Parking: At individual site

Fee: $7

Elevation: 480 feet

Restrictions:

Pets—Allowed on leash

Fires—In fire pits

Alcoholic beverages—At site only

Vehicles—Up to 25 feet; steep and winding road not recommended for large RVs

Other—14-day stay limit; no glass containers in North Sylamore Creek

HAW CREEK FALLS

Pelsor, AR

The word *haw* is old-time mule-driver jargon. The driver would shout "Haw!" to turn his team left and "Gee!" to turn right. Gee Creek runs into Haw Creek near Haw Creek Falls Campground, and at their junction Gee Creek flows from the right and Haw Creek from the left.

No longer is anyone calling mule-team commands or any other shouts in this quiet campground on Haw Creek, a peaceful enclave in the national forest. A thick canopy of hardwoods shades all sites, and walls of trees separate each campsite from its neighbors. Distances between sites are just right, and several sites overlook Haw Creek. Site 6, with excellent privacy and scattered boulders to sit on, is the pick campsite at Haw Creek Falls. The well pump in the campground was recently locked off, and since there's no water, the camping fee was reduced.

Haw Creek Falls Campground is a nice place any time of year, but it's especially beautiful in spring, when the creek's flowing deep. You'll know how it's running when you pull into camp and splash across it on a concrete slab. When the creek is up, the waterfall next to the campground comes alive, lulling you to sleep with its roar. The falls are wide ledges in the creek with several pour-offs and pools. Unless the creek is flooding, it's easy to pick your way out to the middle of the stream to photograph the falls, wade the creek, swim in its two deep

CAMPGROUND RATINGS

Beauty:	★★★★★
Site privacy:	★★★★
Site spaciousness:	★★★
Quiet:	★★★★★
Security:	★★★★
Cleanliness/upkeep:	★★★★★

This campground is next to the 15,000-acre Hurricane Creek Wilderness, which hides a beautiful natural bridge.

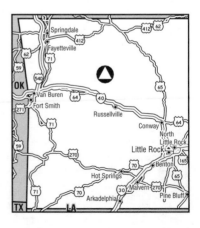

OZARK NATIONAL FOREST

pools, or just laze in the sun on the huge rock slabs in the streambed.

Haw Creek pours into Big Piney Creek a mile downstream from the camp. Bring your raft, whitewater canoe, or kayak and paddle the Class I–III rapids of this Wild and Scenic River. It's an eight-mile trip from AR 123 to Treat and an 18-mile run to Long Pool. Water levels are normally suitable in spring or after downpours. When the creek is too low to boat, try your luck fishing the Big Piney. Not many folks fish

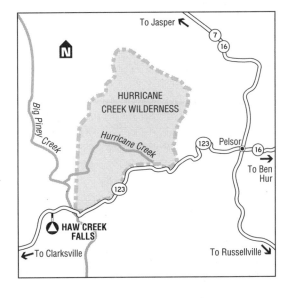

the creek's populations of sunfish, catfish, and several varieties of bass, so the angling is often great. When stream levels are low, you can hike along the creek bed, fishing deep pools and riffles along the Big Piney's meanders.

If you want to see some really cool stuff, get on the Ozark Highlands Trail and make tracks into the Hurricane Creek Wilderness. Covering 15,000 acres north of AR 123 on the east side of Big Piney Creek, this wilderness protects the headwaters of Hurricane Creek and hides a beautiful natural bridge. The bridge is a 6-mile trek from the Big Piney Trailhead, which is a mile east of camp, so save your energy by starting from the trailhead instead of the campground.

Four miles into the wilderness you'll come to a fork. Stay left—the right fork is the high-water route for hikers to avoid Hurricane Creek when it's in flood stage. It misses all the good scenery, including the bridge. A mile down the left fork you'll cross Hurricane Creek, climb to an old road, and turn right to follow it. The trail soon parallels a pretty bluff. Keep your eye on the bluff, and a half mile after crossing Hurricane Creek you'll see the natural bridge high in the cliff.

It's worth the trip just to see the bridge, but don't turn around yet. In the next half mile the trail goes past a huge boulder and back down to Hurricane Creek. There you'll find a beautiful scenic area with backpacker campsites next to the creek and rocks to lounge on while you enjoy the view. It's a perfect spot to relax and snack before heading back to the trailhead.

If you like biking rough, scenic, low-traveled roads, ride the forest service roads around the wilderness. You'll follow Big Piney Creek north on FS 1002/CR 131, fording Hurricane Creek and passing some cool rock outcroppings, to FS 1202/CR 30. Turn right, cross Big Piney Creek, and follow 1202/30 to FS 1209/CR 61. Turn right on 1209/61, ride this rough road down into the valley that once held the community of Chancel, and on to AR 123, where turning right takes you back to Haw Creek Falls. Be in good shape and take a map—there'll be some tough climbs and a few possible wrong turns.

The Ozark Highlands Trail crosses FS 1209 in Chancel. Ditch your bike and take an easy half-mile hike west on the trail to an unbelievably well-crafted rock wall by an old field. As hard as farming must have been back in these deep woods, some homesteader found time to build this impressive wall instead of just piling rocks at his field edge. Amazing.

To get there: From Pelsor on AR 7, drive west 12 miles on AR 123. Haw Creek Falls Campground will be on the south side of the road.

KEY INFORMATION

Haw Creek Falls Campground
Ozark National Forest
12000 SR 27
Hector, AR 72843

Operated by: U.S. Forest Service

Information: (501) 284-3150

Open: Year-round

Individual sites: 9

Each site has: Table, tent pad, fire pit with grate, barbecue grill, lantern pole

Site assignment: First come, first served

Registration: Self pay at loop entrance

Facilities: Vault toilets, trail

Parking: At individual site

Fee: $4

Elevation: 1,000 feet

Restrictions:
   Pets—Allowed on leash
   Fires—In fire pits
   Alcoholic beverages—At site only
   Vehicles—Up to 22 feet
   Other—14-day stay limit; no glass containers in creek

LAKE WEDINGTON

Fayetteville, AR

L ake Wedington Recreation Area, a scenic 102-acre lake in forested hills, is listed on the National Register of Historic Places. The Works Progress Administration built the lake, cabins, and lodge during the 1930s. Fifty years after the site was developed, the recreation area was falling into disrepair, so in 1988 lovers of this scenic historical site formed Friends of Lake Wedington to restore the recreation area to its former splendor. Thanks to their efforts, Lake Wedington today is a recreational jewel in northwest Arkansas.

The campground at Lake Wedington Recreation Area sits on a peninsula between two arms of the lake. It's wisely placed away from the often busy day-use area, separated from the beach and the boat dock by a small bay. You can enjoy the day-use area when you please, and escape to the quiet of your campsite when you want to get away from it all. From many sites you can see the lake through the large canopy of trees that shade the entire campground. Except for sites 2–4, most sites are spaced well apart for good privacy. Site 5 has an especially good view of Lake Wedington. Water faucets are scattered throughout the campground, and rest rooms and showers are in the bathhouse near site 12. A fishing pier near the beginning of the loop is the perfect spot for admiring sunrises and sunsets.

The day-use area is beautiful. A wide, expansive lawn dominated by a rambling stone bathhouse next to the lake makes a

CAMPGROUND RATINGS

Beauty: ★★★★★
Site privacy: ★★★★
Site spaciousness: ★★★★
Quiet: ★★★★
Security: ★★★★
Cleanliness/upkeep: ★★★★★

Lake Wedington Recreation Area, with its 1930s WPA architecture, is on the National Register of Historic Places.

OZARK NATIONAL FOREST

great place to swim, play Frisbee, or laze in the sun. A fascinating old stone diving structure (no longer open for use) stands in the water at the southern end of the swimming area. The beach has two volleyball courts at the edge of the water, and a paved ramp provides wheelchair access to the lake. A concession stand in the bathhouse serves cold drinks, snacks, and ice cream. The old lodge with its stone fireplaces and rustic wood furniture stands on a low hill overlooking the beach. Next to the lodge is a

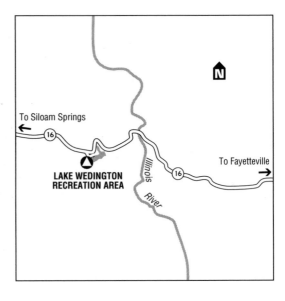

To Siloam Springs

LAKE WEDINGTON
RECREATION AREA

To Fayetteville

Illinois River

shady 19-site picnic area. In season, canoes and paddleboats are for rent at the boathouse. Lake Wedington is a pretty place to canoe, so if you have a canoe, bring it along.

Lake Wedington Recreation Area is graced with two fine trails. The Lakeshore Trail is—you guessed it—a trail around part of the lake's perimeter. This hike goes around the lake's undeveloped east shore, past the rustic and beautiful WPA cabins restored by the Friends of Lake Wedington, through the day-use area, and back to the campground.

The Lake Wedington Trail is an 8-mile tramp through more remote terrain. This hike goes north from a trailhead on the north side of AR 16 between the campground and day-use area entrances. Three miles into the hike you'll climb up through a bluffline and hike a narrow ridge for a short distance, enjoying nice views of the countryside north of Lake Wedington. The trail also passes near both peaks of Twin Mountain, with a half-mile spur leading to the north peak. The spur hike is worth the extra effort—it leads to another wonderful view. The main trail descends to the Illinois River, where it ends. Unless you're going to camp next to the river, it's best to turn around at the peak and head back, thus avoiding the climb from the river bottom.

When you feel like taking it easy, come to Lake Wedington and rent one of the restored cabins. Built with native stone and oak lumber from the trees that once covered the lake bed, these comfortable 60-year-old cabins on the lake's quiet south shore are rustic and remote hideaways.

Lake Wedington Recreation Area

Ozark National Forest

P.O. Box 76, Highway 23 N.
Ozark, AR 72949

Operated by: U.S. Forest Service

Information: (501) 667-2191

Open: Year-round

Individual sites: 18

Each site has: Table, fire pit with grate, lantern pole, tent pad

Site assignment: First come, first served

Registration: Self-pay at loop entrance

Facilities: Water, flush toilets, showers, phone, playground, beach, pavilion, lodge, picnic area, horseshoe pits, beach volleyball courts, cabins, trails

Parking: At individual site

Fee: $8 per site; day-use $2 adult, $1 child; $30 picnic pavilion, $75 lodge

Elevation: 1,140 feet

Restrictions: No Pets Allowed

Pets—Allowed on leash, not allowed on the beach

Fires—In fire pits

Alcoholic beverages—At site only

Vehicles—Up to 32 feet

Other—14-day stay limit

To get there: From US 71 in Fayetteville, drive 13 miles west on AR 16 to the campground entrance. The day-use entrance is a quarter mile west of the campground entrance.

LONG POOL

Dover, AR

L ong Pool Recreation Area is a beautiful place to spend an afternoon or a weekend in the Ozarks. Tucked in the forest next to a natural swimming hole on Big Piney Creek, a designated Wild and Scenic River, Long Pool is a wonderful place for families, floaters, and anglers. Several sites overlook the creek from low bluffs above the swimming hole.

This campground fills on spring weekends when river levels offer good canoeing. It's a popular destination on Memorial Day, Fourth of July, and Labor Day weekends. A loop with water and electricity hookups attracts RVs to this campground, but it's separated from the tent loops to ensure that you won't have someone's generator blowing its noise and fumes into your tent site.

The electric sites, brand new in 2001, are on your left and uphill from the swimming hole as you enter the recreation area. Just upstream from the beach is Loop A, with six campsites next to Big Piney Creek. These camping spots are close together, yet they're popular because they're near the swimming hole and overlook the creek. Sites 3, 4, and 5 are perched on the bluff's edge next to the Big Piney. All these sites are well shaded and have level tent pads.

I like to camp in Loop B, which contains sites 7–19. It's farthest from the swimming hole, but this shady, wooded loop is the quietest place at Long Pool. You can see your neighbors, but the combination of adequate

CAMPGROUND RATINGS

Beauty: ★★★★★
Site privacy: ★★★
Site spaciousness: ★★★
Quiet: ★★★★
Security: ★★★★
Cleanliness/upkeep: ★★★★★

Overlooking a swimming hole on wild and scenic Big Piney Creek, Long Pool is a wonderful place for families and floaters.

OZARK NATIONAL FOREST

spacing and vegetation between sites keeps you from
feeling crowded. Some sites
are nicely terraced into the
hillside a few feet above
road level. My favorites are
sites 8 and 9. They're close
to each other but are spacious and terraced below
road level on a cliff overlooking the stream. You'll
love camping at these level
and shaded sites with a
view of Big Piney Creek.

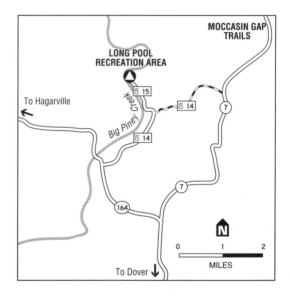

The campground's name-
sake swimming hole is the
big attraction here. It's one
of the best natural swim-
ming pools in the Ozarks. A gravel beach slopes gently into a deep pool in the
creek. A handsome old bathhouse and stone picnic sites are set on the shaded
lawn next to the pool, separated from the gravel bar by a stone retaining wall.
The recreation area's stonework blends well with the fascinating rock outcroppings and bluffs in the Big Piney next to the swimming hole.

For a real getaway, put on your wading shoes, grab your fishing pole, and
head up or downstream. The Big Piney is home to several varieties of bass and
sunfish. It's fun to fish your way along the creek's alternating pools and
rapids. The best angling is in spring and early summer, but you'll find fish in
the creek year-round.

Long Pool is a favorite camp for river runners on this popular float stream.
In either direction from the campground, the Big Piney has something to offer
all levels of boaters. If you prefer adventurous paddling, shuttle upstream to
Helton's Farm Access and make the 10-mile run down to Long Pool. The hills
squeeze the creek into a narrow channel with plenty of rapids. One of the
more exciting rough spots is named Cascades of Extinction.

Rapids leading to extinction are not your idea of fun? Then put in at Long Pool and paddle the more laid-back 5 miles downstream to AR 164. A few easy rapids will make the trip fun, but nothing too intimidating. Whichever part of this creek you float, you'll enjoy views of high mountains, bluffs on the outside of bends, and deep, long pools separated by riffles and rapids. Canoes, shuttles, and information are available at Moore Outdoors, an outfitter whose store you'll pass on your drive in to Long Pool.

If you're a mountain biker, Long Pool makes a great base of operations for exploring the nearby Moccasin Gap trail system. This 28-mile network designed for equestrians is open to bikers and offers some wonderful riding for cyclists of all skill levels. Many trails follow old forest roads, while others are rugged paths on newly cut single-track. To reach the trail system, drive back to the AR 164/AR 7 junction, turn north on AR 7, and go 8 miles north to the trailhead on the left.

Moccasin Gap is a beautiful place to ride. The landscape alone is worth a visit. Trails follow clear streams, climb to breezy ridgetops, and meander through forests of oak and hickory in the bottomlands and stands of pine on the ridges. Especially beautiful is Stave Mill Falls, an exquisite cascade on Stave Mill Creek less than 2 miles from the trailhead.

To get there: From Dover, drive 6 miles north on AR 7 to AR 164. Turn left on AR 164 and drive 3 miles to County Road 14, also known as Old Highway 7. Turn right and drive 3 miles to a fork. The left fork is Long Pool Road. Follow it 2 miles to Long Pool.

KEY INFORMATION

Long Pool Recreation Area
Ozark National Forest
12000 SR 27
Hector, AR 72843

Operated by: U.S. Forest Service

Information: (501) 284-3150

Open: Year-round

Individual sites: 40 single sites, 2 double sites

Each site has: Table, fire pit with grate, lantern pole, tent pad; 22 sites in new loop have water and electricity

Site assignment: First come, first served

Registration: Self-pay at campground entrance

Facilities: Water, flush and vault toilets, showers, picnic shelter, swimming hole with changing room, RV dump, boater access

Parking: At individual site

Fee: $7 basic site, around $12 electric site, $3 per vehicle for day-use, $30 for season pass to day-use area

Elevation: 540 feet

Restrictions:

Pets—Allowed on leash

Fires—In fire pits

Alcoholic beverages—At site only

Vehicles—Up to 40 feet

Other—14-day stay limit; no glass containers on beach or in creek

REDDING

Cass, AR

For scenic beauty and variety of outdoor activities, Redding Campground can't be beat. The Mulberry Wild and Scenic River rolls past this forested camp, waiting to swallow you and your canoe in its rapids. One of the prettiest sections of the Ozark Highlands Trail passes a few miles from Redding, and several excellent mountain bike routes follow little-traveled or abandoned forest roads in the surrounding hills.

Redding Campground is a nice place to be. All sites are well shaded and spacious. Most are separated from neighboring camps by thick woods and brush. They're spaced far enough apart to ensure privacy but close enough to socialize with your neighbors if you want. Water spigots are scattered through the campground, and it's only a short walk to hot showers and flush toilets. The only sites to avoid are 21, 22, and 24—they're packed close together with no brush between them and are across from the bathroom and its all-night lights and squeaking door.

When the river's up, the campground gets busy. People flock to the Mulberry from all over Arkansas to challenge its whitewater. The 16-mile section from Wolf Pen Recreation Area above Redding to Turner Bend below is a very popular stretch for river runners. Dropping 13 to 15 feet per mile on this run, the Mulberry roars through sharp turns, cascades over rock ledges, pushes through strainers and willow thickets, and smashes

CAMPGROUND RATINGS

Beauty: ★★★★
Site privacy: ★★★★★
Site spaciousness: ★★★★★
Quiet: ★★★★
Security: ★★★★
Cleanliness/upkeep: ★★★★★

Redding, with a nearby trail system that connects to the Ozark Highlands Trail, is a hiker's dream.

OZARK NATIONAL FOREST

over boulders. It's a blast to paddle—with a set of rapids named Whoop and Holler, how could it ever be boring? Water levels are usually suitable from late fall to early June.

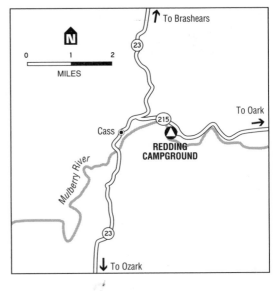

If river running isn't for you, bring your mountain bike. You can ride 23-mile Spy Rock Trail from camp. It climbs up onto Morgan and Hare Mountains on well-maintained Morgan Mountain Road/FS 1504, follows a very high ridge for several miles, and then returns to AR 215 on rough, rugged FS 1533. One and a half miles up Morgan Mountain Road you can ditch your bike and hike a quarter-mile spur trail to Spy Rock, where you'll admire a vista of the Mulberry River Valley. On FS 1533 you'll pass an old chimney and foundation, all that remains of a long-gone homestead.

For a less technical ride, drive over to Turner Bend, park at the store, and pedal the 18-mile Ragtown Road Loop. This ride won't require expert bike-handling skills, but you'll not get off easy. It has some *long* climbs—but those climbs translate into scenic views, so it's worth the huffing and puffing. On the loop you can visit Gray's Spring, a mountainside picnic area, and pedal through Bee Rock, where the road squeaks between two huge stone formations.

For a real technical challenge, take your bike over to the Mill Creek ATV area south of Combs. This 42-mile trail system features a 27-mile main loop interlaced with 15 miles of interior loops and connectors. It varies from laid-back cruises on ridges and streamsides to thigh-burning climbs and white-knuckle descents. Except for the easy Burrel Mountain Loop, Mill Creek is only for strong and experienced riders.

For hikers, Redding is a dream. The Redding–Spy Rock Loop leaves from a trailhead a half mile east of the campground. This 9-mile loop climbs the side of Morgan Mountain to Spy Rock Vista and returns, passing several small waterfalls along the way. Near Spy Rock a connector runs over to the Ozark Highlands Trail, tying you into nearly 200 miles of scenic wandering.

The 19-mile section of the Ozark Highlands Trail between Cherry Bend on AR 23 and Lick Branch Trailhead on County Road 33 is gorgeous. It goes right over 2,380-foot Hare Mountain, the highest point on this 175-mile trail. An old well and a haunting rock wall are all that remains of a farm that once worked this flat-topped mountain. The old wall is an ideal seat for admiring the valley of the Mulberry and surrounding Boston Mountains fading into the distant smoky blue haze. The rest of this section of trail travels bluff edges, splashes through streams, skirts waterfalls on Indian Creek, and passes through the Marinoni Scenic Area, a fantastic little canyon not far from Lick Branch.

For an easy hike to the peak of Hare Mountain, use the Hare Mountain Trailhead 4 miles up Morgan Mountain Road from AR 215. From there it's only a 2-mile hike on a razorback ridge to the top of Hare Mountain.

KEY INFORMATION

Redding Campground
Ozark National Forest
P.O. Box 190
AR Highway 21 N.
Clarksville, AR 72830

Operated by: U.S. Forest Service

Information: (501) 754-2864

Open: Year-round

Individual sites: 25

Each site has: Table, tent pad, fire pit with grate, lantern pole

Site assignment: First come, first served

Registration: Self-pay station at loop entrance

Facilities: Water, flush toilets, showers, river access, trails

Parking: At individual site

Fee: $10 per site, $3 for parking and river access use, $2 for use of shower only

Elevation: 760 feet

Restrictions:

Pets—Allowed on leash

Fires—In fire pits

Alcoholic beverages—At site only

Vehicles—Up to 35 feet

Other—14-day stay limit; no glass containers in river

To get there: From Ozark, drive 18 miles north on AR 23 to AR 215. Drive 3 miles east on AR 215 to the campground on the south side of the highway.

RICHLAND CREEK

Ben Hur, AR

Located 9 miles from the nearest paved road, Richland Creek is a rustic little campground that packs quite an outdoor punch. There are trails to hike, a wonderful swimming hole, wilderness waterfalls to explore, and winding, hilly forest roads to mountain bike. Even the drive into the campground is wonderful—FS 1205 is called Falling Water Road, and you'll know why if you make the drive when the creeks are flowing.

Richland Creek is a kind of disorganized little place, but that's part of its charm. Campsites are a little scattered and don't all have the same amenities. Three sites are next to the creek. For campers who like being near water they're great, but they have no grass around them—just gravel and packed dirt, with only a table and a fire pit. I prefer the sites on the bench above the creek. The first of these sites has only a table and a fire pit, but it's in a nice grassy spot off the entrance road. My favorites are the six sites beyond the pump house. They have all the amenities, and the first three are private sites set back in their own little clearings in the forest. The last three sites are at the end of the road, evenly spaced in a shady open area a few steps from Falling Water Creek.

This free campground often fills on weekends from spring through fall, and on holiday weekends it's jammed. Avoid the first week of October, when an equestrian trail

CAMPGROUND RATINGS

Beauty: ★★★★★
Site privacy: ★★★
Site spaciousness: ★★★★
Quiet: ★★★★★
Security: ★★★★
Cleanliness/upkeep: ★★★

A 3-mile hike west from the campground is Twin Falls, possibly the most beautiful waterfall in the Ozarks.

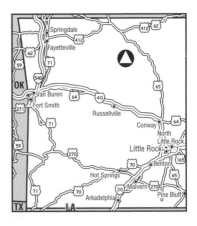

OZARK NATIONAL FOREST

ride takes over the camp, as well as the following week, when an ATV group has a rally at Richland Creek. Unlike most forest service–run campgrounds, this one allows camping anywhere—even outside specific sites—so it can get a little crazy at times. Plan accordingly and visit Richland Creek during the week or off-season. Most folks come to hike deep into the Richland Creek Wilderness immediately west of camp and check out Twin Falls.

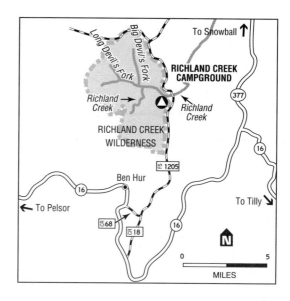

There's no official trail to the falls—just a mishmash of paths following Richland Creek into the wilderness. Just go to the end of the lower campground, cross Falling Water Creek, and start working your way upstream along the south side of Richland Creek. It's about 3 challenging miles to the falls, but it's so scenic that you'll love the trek. When Richland Creek takes a hard turn from the south, with another creek pouring in from the far side, you're in fantastic scenery. If you continue upstream on Richland Creek another half mile, you'll find a waterfall where the creek pours over a 100-foot-wide ledge.

Devil's Fork, that other stream pouring into Richland Creek, has the even more spectacular Twin Falls. A quarter mile upstream from Devil's Fork's junction with Richland Creek, Big Devil's Fork and Long Devil's Fork come together as an incredibly beautiful pair of waterfalls, pouring into a broad pool from opposite sides of a low bluff. These falls are broad, 15-foot-tall curtains pouring off deeply undercut ledges.

More hiking awaits you on the Ozark Highlands Trail. It comes to Richland from the south and heads east. I like the 8-mile stretch of trail from Richland

Creek to the Stack Rock Trailhead on FS 1201. You'll not see anything as spectacular as Twin Falls, but it's a pretty hike with vistas of the Richland Creek Valley, house-sized boulders, rugged rock gardens, and exquisite little streams with pools and small waterfalls. If you're really energetic, or can have someone shuttle you, hike the Ozark Highlands Trail clear to Woolum Ford on the Buffalo National River.

The best way to get to Woolum Ford is by mountain bike. It's 19 miles via FS 1205, FS 1201, and the county road heading north from the old townsite of Eula. You'll have a stiff climb and an exhilarating descent each way, two fords of Richland Creek, and lots of pretty scenery. As you approach the Buffalo in the Richland Creek Valley, a rock wall rises on your left. Ditch your bike and find your way up the rock wall and you'll be standing on The Nars, a causeway-like stone with the Buffalo rolling by on the other side. At places The Nars are only a few feet wide.

There's a nice 40-mile mountain bike loop leading from Richland Creek to Woolum, then returning via county and forest roads. It goes through the Cave Creek valley, past the old community of Bass, and along the north and east sides of the Richland Creek Wilderness. Lots of intersections make it confusing in places, but it's well worth the effort.

To get there: From Pelsor at the junction of AR 7, AR 123, and AR 16, drive 8 miles east on AR 16 to Forest Road 1205, 1 mile past Ben Hur. Turn left on FS 1205/County Road 68 and follow it 8.5 miles to Richland Creek Campground on the left side of the road. It's easy to miss the turn on FS 1205. If you do, go 2 miles farther on AR 16, and turn left onto FS 1313/County Road 18. It goes past the Falling Water Church and joins FS 1205 to the campground.

KEY INFORMATION

Richland Creek Campground
Ozark National Forest
P.O. Box 427, Highway 7 N.
Jasper, AR 72641

Operated by: U.S. Forest Service

Information: (870) 446-5122

Open: Year-round

Individual sites: 10

Each site has: Site near entrance and 3 sites next to creek only have table and fire pit with grate; sites on bench above the creeks have table, fire pit with grate, fire ring with two benches, lantern pole

Site assignment: First come, first served

Registration: No registration required

Facilities: Vault toilets, trails, water; faucet water must be purified; water turned off November through March

Parking: At individual site

Fee: Donations accepted at box near entrance

Elevation: 1,000 feet

Restrictions:

Pets—Allowed on leash

Fires—In fire pits and fire rings only

Alcoholic beverage—At campsite only

Vehicles—Up to 25 feet

Other—14-day stay limit; no glass containers in creek

SHORES LAKE

Mulberry, AR

S hores Lake is 82 acres of sky blue beauty deep in the Boston Mountains of northwest Arkansas. The dam was begun by the CCC in the 1930s, but left unfinished until 1958, when the forest service and Arkansas Fish and Game Commission completed the project. Now Shores Lake is a popular camping, fishing, and swimming destination at the end of the pavement in the Ozark National Forest. You might not want to camp here if you're superstitious—there's an old cemetery next to site 1—but less timid campers will love spending a few nights in this wooded lakeside retreat.

The campground is located at the upper end of the Shores Lake. It's a pretty set of campsites in a double loop under a canopy of hardwoods and pines. The tent pads at each site are outlined with native stone, and every site is level and shady. While there are many trees shading the campground, there is little ground-level brush between the sites to create privacy. Spacing between sites is tight. Sites 7 and 8 are closest to the lake, and site 8 has nice views of the water. Site 12, off by itself on a low rise above the rest of the campground, has the most privacy, but it has the least shade of any site at Shores Lake.

The lake is a wonderful place to while away a warm summer afternoon. A grassy field sloping from the bathhouse to the water's edge is a fine place to play Frisbee or nap on your blanket in the sun. A dip in the lake is only a few steps away. In the

CAMPGROUND RATINGS

Beauty: ★★★★
Site privacy: ★★
Site spaciousness: ★★★
Quiet: ★★★★
Security: ★★★★
Cleanliness/upkeep: ★★★★★

Shores Lake is a beautiful Ozark Lake nestled under the ramparts of White Rock Mountain.

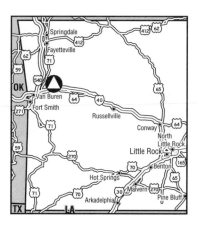

OZARK NATIONAL FOREST

woods behind the bathhouse there are 28 beautiful picnic sites on a spur road running along a little highland between the day-use area and the campground.

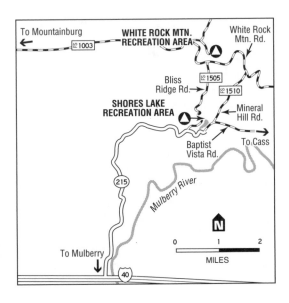

Bring the fishing tackle—Shores Lake is stocked with bass, catfish, and bluegill. Two fishing piers near the swimming area have underwater structures to attract fish. The biggest fish stick to the middle of the lake, so you'll have more success if you bring a canoe or boat (10 hp motor limit). Whether you fish or paddle around, you'll have fun exploring the lake by boat.

If you like adventurous canoeing, plan to float the lower portions of the nearby Mulberry River. From Turner Bend on AR 23 west of Shores Lake, it's a 10-mile run to Campbell Cemetery on Forest Road 1501. Another exciting trip is the 13-mile float from Campbell Cemetery to the Mill Creek access south of Shores Lake. The wild and scenic Mulberry will challenge you with Class II whitewater, willow thickets, and strainers as it tumbles through the Boston Mountains. The Mulberry is normally floatable from late fall to June. Canoe rentals and shuttles are available at Turner Bend.

If you'd rather hike than paddle, you're in luck. A trailhead for the Shores Lake–White Rock Mountain Loop is at the north edge of the campground. On this 15-mile hike you'll climb to the peak of White Rock Mountain, gaining 1,600 feet of altitude on the way to its 2,260-foot summit. If the weather's been wet, you'll cross numerous streams and pass several waterfalls on your way to and from the peak. On its way to White Rock the loop uses part of the Ozark Highlands Trail. On the mountaintop you'll relax in cool highland breezes and admire the surrounding countryside before starting the easy descent back to Shores Lake.

The forest roads north and east of Shores Lake are wonderful routes for exploring the hills on your mountain bike. Riding 13 miles east of Shores Lake on Baptist Vista Road (FS 1501) takes you to Turner Bend, where you can cool off with a cold drink at the store. This gravel road passes a beautiful overlook above Shores Lake. From Turner Bend you can return through the highlands on FS 1003 (White Rock Road), pedaling through Bee Rock and past Gray's Spring, and descending back to FS 1501 on any of the several forest roads that connect it to FS 1003.

If you choose FS 1512 for your descent, look for a faint road leading west near its junction with FS 1514. It leads to a cemetery in the woods, with graves from the mid-1800s to around 1900. Repeated epitaphs stating "Died at Birth" testify how hard life once was in these Boston Mountains. A map of the Ozark National Forest and the book *Mountain Bike! The Ozarks*, written by Steve Henry (see the Bibliography on page 168), will help you find this cemetery and the numerous mountain biking routes around Shores Lake.

Though Shores Lake is a remote hideaway in the Boston Mountains, it's a popular destination on summer weekends. If it's too busy, head for the hills on White Rock Mountain. The campground there is rarely full, and it's usually cooler on the mountaintop, 1,600 feet above Shores Lake.

To get there: From Mulberry, drive 15 miles north on AR 215 to Forest Service Road 1505/Bliss Ridge Road. Turn left on Bliss Ridge Road and drive a half mile to Shores Lake. The campground entrance is a quarter mile past the day-use area.

KEY INFORMATION

Shores Lake Recreation Area Ozark National Forest P.O. Box 76, AR Highway 23 N. Ozark, AR 72949

Operated by: U.S. Forest Service

Information: (501) 667-2191

Open: Year-round

Individual sites: 23

Each site has: Table, fire pit with grate, lantern pole, tent pad

Site assignment: First come, first served

Registration: Self-pay at campground entrance

Facilities: Water, flush and vault toilets, showers, pavilion, beach, picnic area, boat ramp, fishing piers, trail; water, showers, and flush toilets turned off in winter

Parking: At individual site

Fee: $8 per site, $3 per vehicle for day-use area; half-price November–March when water is turned off

Elevation: 675 feet

Restrictions:

Pets—Allowed on leash

Fires—In fire pits

Alcoholic beverages—At site only

Vehicles—Up to 22 feet

Other—14-day stay limit; no glass containers on beach

Loud parties in October on weekends!

135

SPRING LAKE

Belleville, AR

Spring Lake is a little-known hideaway in the Magazine District of the Ozark National Forest. The first time I went there I had no idea what to expect. In years of travel around the Ozarks I'd never heard of it, so I figured it couldn't be that great.

I couldn't have been more wrong. Spring Lake, another of the 1930s Civilian Conservation Corps projects gracing the Ozark hills, is one of the prettiest recreation areas in Arkansas. A stone bathhouse overlooks a grassy hillside sloping to a sandy beach. Shady picnic sites are scattered across the hillside, and wide stairs descend from the bathhouse to the lakeshore. Massive diving platforms rise from the lake in the swimming area. The platforms, bathhouse, picnic sites, and stairs all showcase beautiful CCC-era stonework construction.

The campground, next to 82-acre Spring Lake, is just as beautiful as the day-use area. It's across the lake from the beach, so you can admire this picturesque old CCC recreation site from the peace and quiet of your camp. Stonework terracing around tables and tent pads at some campsites mirror the CCC architecture across the lake. Huge pines and hardwoods shade this pretty campground. Their cover, plus dips in the nearby lake, will cool you on the hottest summer day.

Spring Lake lies off the beaten path on gravel roads. The campground rarely fills, even on holiday weekends. I wish it was a

CAMPGROUND RATINGS

Beauty:	★★★★★
Site privacy:	★★★★★
Site spaciousness:	★★★★★
Quiet:	★★★★★
Security:	★★★★
Cleanliness/upkeep:	★★★★★

Spring Lake, perhaps the prettiest campground in the Ozark National Forest, is a little-visited gem at the foot of Mt. Magazine.

OZARK NATIONAL FOREST

little more popular, so that this attractive yet little-known camp would open year-round. Its sites are scattered along the lakeshore on either side of a pavilion on a dead-end road. Sites 1–8 are far apart in deep woods on the east side of the pavilion, offering the most seclusion. Sites 5, 7, and 8 have the prettiest views of the lake. Sites 9–13, west of the pavilion, also overlook the water but are crowded together in a more open area.

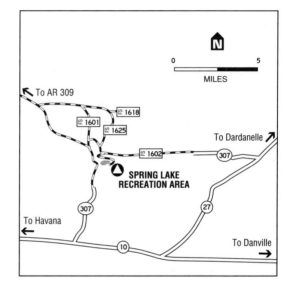

The atmosphere at Spring Lake is laid-back and calm, perfect for hanging out in camp or at the beach, reading a good book, and listening to the breeze sigh through the pines shading your lawn chair. You can toss horseshoes over by the pavilion. If you have enough companions, you can play volleyball there, too. The Spring Lake Trail, an easy 2-mile path exploring the lake's east shore and the low hills surrounding it, starts near the shelter.

Mountain bikers can use Spring Lake as a base for exploring the nearby Huckleberry Mountain Horse Trail. This 34-mile trail system consists of three loops ranging in length from 9 to 18 miles. Though designed for horses, it's a wonderful network for mountain biking, with options for riders of all skill levels. From the 10.4-mile Apple Loop, you can ride a 1-mile spur to a scenic overlook on AR 309 near the top of Mt. Magazine.

A good starting point for the northern part of the trail system is the top of Huckleberry Mountain. To get there, drive 6 miles west of Spring Lake on FS 1601 to FS 1613, then go north 4 miles on FS 1613 to Huckleberry Trail Camp. This camp, with its high mountain meadow, pretty spring-fed lake, and great views of the surrounding area, is worth the trip all by itself.

From Huckleberry Mountain you can pedal circuits of 9, 15, and 18 miles on the Huckleberry Mountain portion of the trail system. The 9-mile loop, a cut-off portion of the 18-mile option, is an easy ride on the shoulders of the mountain. It has several good vistas of the Arkansas River valley to the north, and it also makes a wonderful hike. The 15-mile loop has some very technical sections but follows old woods double-tracks for most of its length. The loop parallels Shoal Creek on its west side, showcasing several beautiful waterfalls and rapids when the creek is running. Riding the entire perimeter of the Huckleberry Loop gives you a challenging 18-mile ride.

To access the Apple Loop, drive 8 miles west of Spring Lake to Shoal Creek. Find the trail markers just east of the creek, and you'll be at the junction of the Apple and Huckleberry Loops. The 10.4-mile Apple Loop goes south and west from here. Just west of this trailhead the trail crosses Shoal Creek on a waterfall ledge. Don't wimp out and skip the 1.5-mile spur leading to the 2,753-foot peak of Mt. Magazine on the Apple Loop's west side. The scenic vistas from Arkansas' newest state park make the climb worth every bit of huffing and puffing.

To get there: From Dardanelle, drive 9 miles southwest on AR 27 to AR 307. Turn west on AR 307. After 3 miles, AR 307 becomes gravel Forest Service Road 1602. Continue an additional 4 miles on FS 1602 to Spring Lake. From Belleville, drive north on AR 307. After 4 miles the road becomes gravel FS 1602. Continue an additional 3 miles to Spring Lake.

KEY INFORMATION

Spring Lake Recreation Area Ozark National Forest
P.O. Box 511, 3001 E. Walnut
Paris, AR 72855

Operated by: U.S. Forest Service

Information: (501) 963-3076

Open: May 23–September 2

Individual sites: 13

Each site has: Table, tent pad, fire pit with grate, lantern pole, barbecue grill

Site assignment: First-come, first-served

Registration: Self-pay at campground entrance

Facilities: Water, pavilion, boat ramp, beach, showers and flush toilets at beach, vault toilets in campground, picnic area, horseshoe pits

Parking: At individual site

Fee: $7 per site, $3 per vehicle in day-use areas

Elevation: 520 feet

Restrictions:

Pets—Allowed on leash

Fires—In fire pits

Alcoholic beverages—At site only

Vehicles—Up to 25 feet

Other—14-day stay limit; no glass containers on beach

WHITE ROCK MOUNTAIN

Mulberry, AR

Y ou don't often get to camp on top of a
mountain without hiking there. Even
more seldom do you enjoy incredible mountaintop vistas just a short walk from your
campsite. Both of these pleasures are yours
at White Rock Mountain, though you'll
have to drive 10 miles of gravel roads to get
there. You can see for miles during the day
and enjoy cooling high-country breezes at
night. It's 1,600 feet higher than the surrounding lowlands and on the top of the
2,260-foot White Rock Mountain is always
a bit cooler.

White Rock is historical as well as beautiful. Its lodge, cabins, and trail shelters were
built by the Civilian Conservation Corps in
the 1930s. Over the years these rustic structures weathered badly. In 1987 the Friends of
White Rock was formed to renovate the
structures, and the renovation work finished
in 1991. The old stone and wood cabins with
rock fireplaces and original furniture can be
rented year-round.

Though this sounds like a commercial-
ized place, it's really not. The nearest town
is 17 miles away, and dirt roads sort out
those who hate dust and bumps. The campground is on the right as you drive into the
area, and the picnic area is 100 yards beyond. Each site has a stone-lined tent pad
and is set well away from its neighbors.
While there are enough trees to provide
some shade for each site, the mountaintop's
thin forest with little underbrush means all

CAMPGROUND RATINGS

Beauty:	★★★★★
Site privacy:	★★★
Site spaciousness:	★★★★★
Quiet:	★★★★★
Security:	★★★★
Cleanliness/upkeep:	★★★★

*White Rock Mountain is
a wonderful place to
admire Ozark sunsets.*

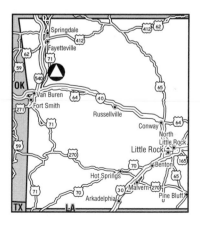

OZARK NATIONAL FOREST

your neighbors are visible. But that's okay because this small campground doesn't feel cramped even when it's full. Sites 1–4 are between the loop and the White Rock entrance road. I prefer sites 5–8. They are on the outside of the loop, away from the road. From these sites you get hints of views through the trees, and the tent pads are set a short way down the hill for a bit more privacy.

It's nice to hang out in the campground at White Rock and listen to the mountain breezes as they sift through

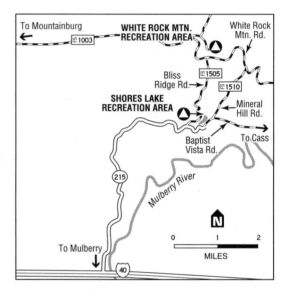

the treetops. If you walk over to the picnic area and down the short spur to the trail shelter built on the cliff's edge, you can enjoy a 270-degree panorama. This shelter is a wonderful place to watch the sunset. Arrows painted on top of the wall point to local towns and give their distances from the mountaintop. At sunset, just before the overlook closes, you can see the lights of each town.

To check out all the views from the peak, hike the 2.1-mile White Rock Rim Loop. It's an easy, level hike all the way around the mountaintop, with vistas almost all the way. This hike's official start is at the trailhead at the end of the cabin road, but you can pick it up from the picnic area overlook, too. A mile north from the trailhead is the first of four trail shelters. This overlook is a fantastic place to greet the sunrise. Looping around to the west side there is another shelter that's only a short distance from the campground loop. Just beyond this shelter a couple of paths lead up to camp. The only drawback to this incredible hike is safety—do not bring your children on this hike. It follows the bluff-line for most of its length, and one slip could be fatal. A sign on the entrance road warns, "Watch Children—6 Have Fallen to Death."

White Rock is also part of the 14-mile Shores Lake–White Rock Mountain Loop. This tough trail gains 1,700 feet coming up from Shores Lake. It makes a perfect weekend hike. You can set up camp or stash your gear in a rented cabin on White Rock Mountain, then drive back to Shores Lake. Leave your car there and enjoy the steep climb without a pack, spend a night on the mountain, and head back to Shores Lake the next day.

A 38-mile mountain bike route shows all the forested beauty between White Rock Mountain and Cass, 16 miles east of the peak. Follow the ups and downs of FS 1003/White Rock Mountain Road all the way to Cass. On the way you can stop at Gray's Spring, a pretty mountainside picnic area. A short way past Gray's Spring the road squeezes through Bee Rock and then descends 2.5 miles to AR 23 at Cass. A 1-mile side trip south on AR 23 is the Turner Bend store, where you can buy a sandwich and have a picnic next to the Mulberry River. Ride back to White Rock Mountain on Forest Roads 1520, 1506, 1007, and 1505, passing some cool rock outcroppings on FS 1505. The trip back can be confusing, so buy a forest map or trail guide at the Turner Bend Store.

To get there: Fom Mulberry, drive north 15 miles on AR 215 to Forest Road 1505/Bliss Ridge Road. Turn left on Bliss Ridge Road and go north 8 miles to FS 1003/White Rock Mountain Road. Turn left on White Rock Mountain Road and drive 1.5 miles to FS 1505/Hurricane Road. Turn right on Hurricane Road and drive 1 mile to the White Rock Mountain Recreation Area entrance.

KEY INFORMATION

White Rock Mountain Recreation Area
Ozark National Forest
P.O. Box 76, AR Highway 23 N. Ozark, AR 72949

Operated by: U.S. Forest Service

Information: (501) 667-2191

Open: Year-round

Individual sites: 8

Each site has: Table, tent pad, fire pit with grate, lantern pole

Site assignment: First come, first served

Registration: Pay at white house just south of campground

Facilities: Vault toilets, water, trail, picnic area; water turned off November–March

Parking: At individual site

Fee: $5

Elevation: 2,250 feet

Restrictions:

Pets—Allowed on leash

Fires—In fire pits

Alcoholic beverages—At campsite only

Vehicles—Up to 22 feet

Other—14-day stay limit; overlooks and rim trail closed at sunset

OUACHITA NATIONAL FOREST

ALBERT PIKE

Langley, AR

A lbert Pike Recreation Area is named for a Confederate general who once lived on the river nearby. This popular campground's sites are a little too close together, but Albert Pike's setting is so pretty and offers so much to do that I included it anyway. Tucked into a bend of the Little Missouri Wild and Scenic River under a steep bluff rising above the campground, Albert Pike is hidden away in forested mountain country that many consider the most beautiful in Arkansas.

General Pike was run out of the country when bushwhackers torched his cabin, but nowadays the atmosphere along the Little Missouri is quite a bit more congenial. Even though sites are close together, folks camping at Albert Pike are usually friendly and laid-back. The campground is divided into Areas A, B, and C. Areas A and B are closed during winter, but C is open year-round. Area A has 11 sites close to the swimming hole, with a few really nice spots overlooking the Little Missouri. Area A's drawback is that it also serves as access road to an RV park on private property outside the national forest, resulting in some annoying pass-through traffic.

Area B is across Forest Road 106 from A. It's a pretty place with nine campsites hugging the bluff that overlooks the campground, but its sites are the most crowded of the three areas. The Little Missouri Trailhead is at Area B's entrance, and the trail passes through the camp. Area C, strung

CAMPGROUND RATINGS

Beauty: ★★★★★
Site privacy: ★★
Site spaciousness: ★★
Quiet: ★★★★
Security: ★★★★
Cleanliness/upkeep: ★★★★★

Many consider the forested mountains around Albert Pike to be the most beautiful country in Arkansas

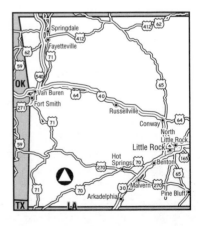

144

OUACHITA NATIONAL FOREST

along both sides of FS 73, is the best. FS 73 has occasional traffic, but pavement through the camp area eliminates the dust and that annoying gravel-crunching tire noise. In Area C sites are not so crowded together and are a little more spacious. A brand-new shower house serves these 24 campsites next to the river. Sites on the south side of the road are next to the stream. Set away from its neighbors with good privacy, site 20 in Area C is the pick site at Albert Pike.

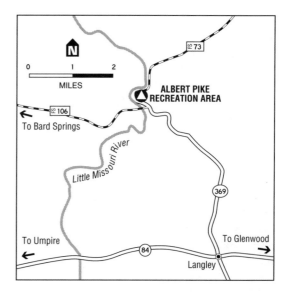

After the swimming hole, the biggest attraction near Albert Pike is Little Missouri Falls. To reach it, drive 3 miles northeast from camp on FS 73 to FS 43, then northwest 4.5 miles to FS 25, then west 1 mile to Little Missouri Falls Picnic Area. The falls are an incredible place, with a big waterfall, several small cascades, and overlook platforms for admiring the river's beauty. In summer it's a perfect place to sit in the deep pool while the cool water splashes on your head.

The 15-mile Little Missouri Trail, the most scenic hike in the Ouachitas, runs right through the camp. Open to both hiking and mountain biking, its northern trailhead is 3 miles west of Little Missouri Falls. From there it's 4 miles to Little Missouri Falls and 10 miles to Albert Pike, with four crossings of the Little Missouri, several splashing fords of its tributaries, and several good overlooks and swimming holes along the way. Just before the trail reaches Area B, you'll see Rock Springs gurgling out of the base of a monstrous rock that towers above the path.

The best part of the Little Missouri Trail runs southwest from Albert Pike. From the trailhead at Area B you'll climb up a series of switchbacks. Near the top of the climb a spur trail breaks right off the main route and goes a few hundred feet to some unique rock out-croppings that look like castle battle-ments. Peek through one of the gaps for a spectacular vista overlooking Albert Pike Recreation Area 300 feet below. From this vista the trail trends downhill for 2 miles to the Winding Stairs Trailhead on FS 106, 2 road miles west of the campground.

If you don't do any other hiking or bik-ing at Albert Pike, absolutely do not miss the southernmost 3 miles of the Little Missouri Trail. They take you through the Winding Stairs, one of the most scenic spots in the state. In the Stairs, where for a half mile the trail passes huge boulders, rock domes, cascades, waterfalls, and bluffs dotted with pines, you'll think you're in Colorado. Calm, clear pools between the cascades form deep swimming holes to cool you on summer trips to the Winding Stairs.

Most people turn around at the Stairs, thinking it'll be hard to top the beauty of this rugged enclave. Push on past the Stairs, though—the trail becomes easy and level in the widening river bottom, and a mile later you'll reach the end of the Little Missouri Trail and a special reward—a crystal-clear 15-foot-deep hole with a rope swing that will dump you happily in the deepest part of the river.

KEY INFORMATION

**Albert Pike Recreation Area
Ouachita National Forest
912 Smokey Bear Lane
Glenwood, AR 71943**

Operated by: U.S. Forest Service

Information: (870) 356-4186

Open: Year-round (Area C)

Individual sites: 46

Each site has: Table, fire pit with grate, lantern pole; some sites have tent pad

Site assignment: First come, first served

Registration: Self-pay at area entrances

Facilities: Water, flush and vault toilets, showers, trails

Parking: At individual site

Fee: $10

Elevation: 900 feet

Restrictions:

Pets—Allowed on leash; not allowed in swimming area

Fires—In fire grates

Alcoholic beverages—At camp-site only

Vehicles—Up to 24 feet

Other—14-day stay limit; no glass containers in river or at swimming hole

To get there: Take AR 369 6 miles north-west of Langley. The highway ends at the campground entrance.

BARD SPRINGS

Athens, AR

B ard Springs was named for a homesteader from nearby Shady Lake. Ac-
cording to local legend, he discovered the
crystal-clear spring that tumbles into Blaylock Creek in this recreation area. Locals
also believe the water gurgling from Bard
Spring had medicinal properties. For years
folks traveled many miles over rough
roads to fill their jugs at this peaceful enclave in the Ouachita Mountains.

Before the 1900s Bard Springs was accessible only by horse. In the 1930s the Civilian
Conservation Corps built a bathhouse and
two dams on Blaylock Creek just upstream
from the spring. The handsome stone bathhouse, listed on the National Register of
Historic Places, still stands above the spring.
It's closed due to water-quality problems,
but the forest service plans to restore it to its
original condition and reopen it as a changing house for folks enjoying the swimming
hole at Bard Springs.

Bard Springs Recreation Area is an under-
used gem. When nearby Albert Pike Recreation Area is filled to overflowing, you'll
still find a quiet camping spot here. Loop A
has five campsites on a loop near the bathhouse and swimming hole on Blaylock
Creek. Site 5 in the middle of the loop isn't
that great, but the others are excellent. Sites
1 and 2 are on the rise above one of the
stone dams, and sites 3 and 4 are down
next to Blaylock Creek. All sites are spacious, level, shady, and secluded.

CAMPGROUND RATINGS

Beauty: ★★★★
Site privacy: ★★★★
Site spaciousness: ★★★★
Quiet: ★★★★★
Security: ★★★★
Cleanliness/upkeep: ★★★★★

*Believing Bard Spring's clean
and cool water to have
medicinal qualities, folks once
traveled from miles around to fill
their jugs at this little spring
in the Ouachita Mountains.*

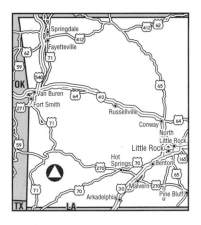

OUACHITA NATIONAL FOREST

Loop B is across Blaylock Creek from the bathhouse and is nicely shaded by deep woods. It's the place to be in foul weather—five of its seven sites have three-sided shelters called Adirondacks. These sheds are perfect for riding out rainstorms. They are also nice for people like me who don't like putting up tents. When money becomes available, Adirondacks will be constructed for the other two sites.

These shelters do have their hazards. I once rolled out my sleeping bag at Bard Springs and snoozed away a rainy night, lulled by the raindrops pattering on my Adirondack's roof. Apparently I wasn't the only one enjoying the dry space—when I awoke the next morning and knocked my boots over, a skunk skittered from under my shelter, ran past the neighbor's tent, and slipped under their car. Getting close to nature has its risks.

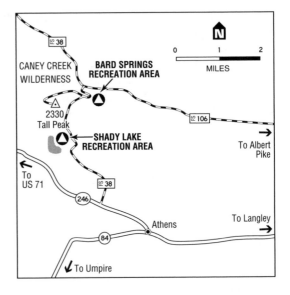

With or without the skunks, Bard Springs is a sweet place to spend a week-end. The swimming hole is fine for a dip, and Blaylock Creek is a neat little stream for wading and exploring. Three miles to the southwest is Tall Peak, where you can admire the surrounding countryside from a fire lookout at 2,330 feet. Looking south, you'll see the blue jewel of Shady Lake tucked in the valley of Saline Creek.

Hikers and mountain bikers will love Bard Springs. The Viles Branch Equestrian Trail, an excellent mountain bike ride suitable for riders of all skill levels, goes right past the campground. On this winding 24-mile route you'll fol-low FS 106 along Blaylock Creek to the Winding Stairs trailhead and then turn south to pedal through the incredibly scenic Winding Stairs of the Little Missouri

River. Just south of the Stairs you'll pick up an old road next to Viles Branch and follow it west, splashing through lots of stream fords, ending up at FS 38 near Shady Lake. From there you'll return to Bard Springs via Forest Roads 38 and 106.

If you like tough hikes, check out the nearby Athens–Big Fork Trail. This steep and rugged path follows a 100-year-old mail route between Athens and Big Fork. Folks were tough back then—this route climbs steeply over eight mountains on its 10-mile run across the Ouachita ridge-tops. Spectacular vistas from several of the mountaintops make the trip well worth the effort.

The Athens–Big Fork trail can be combined with segments of the Viles Branch and Little Missouri Trails for a 27-mile route called the Eagle Rock Loop. If you complete this scenic but challenging ramble through the Ouachitas, head over to the Caddo Ranger District. They'll give you a commemorative patch and list your name with other hikers who've met the challenge of the Eagle Rock Loop.

The Caney Creek Wilderness 1 mile west of Bard Springs has 14 miles of trail and almost 15,000 acres of wild country for you to explore. To get to the Caney Creek Trailhead, go west 1 mile to FS 38, then north a quarter mile to the Caney Creek Trailhead. To hike a 9-mile loop in this beautiful wilderness, walk a mile north from this trailhead on FS 38 to the Buckeye Trailhead. From there you can hike the Buckeye Trail 5 miles southwest to the Caney Creek Trail, then follow it back to your car.

> **To get there:** From Athens, go northwest 2 miles on AR 246 to FS 38. Turn north and follow FS 38 8 miles to FS 106. Turn east and follow FS 106 1 mile to Bard Springs.

KEY INFORMATION

Bard Springs Recreation Area
Ouachita National Forest
912 Smokey Bear Lane
Glenwood, AR 71943

Operated by: U.S. Forest Service

Information: (870) 356-4186

Open: Year-round

Individual sites: 12

Each site has: Table, fire pit with grate, lantern pole; most sites in Loop A have tent pads, most sites in Loop B have Adirondack-style shelters

Site assignment: First come, first served

Registration: Self-pay at loop entrances

Facilities: Vault toilets, picnic shelter, swimming hole

Parking: At individual site

Fee: $5

Elevation: 1,280 feet

Restrictions:

Pets—Allowed on leash

Fires—In fire pits

Alcoholic beverages—At site only

Vehicles—Up to 24 feet; rough and steep roads to Bard Springs unsuitable for RVs or trailers

Other—14-day stay limit, no glass containers in swimming area

CHARLTON

Crystal Springs, AR

Charlton Recreation Area is a wonderful combination of the luxurious and the rustic. A native stone dam on Walnut Creek forms one of the most picturesque swimming holes in Arkansas. The spring-fed creek waters keep the pool cool and clear on the hottest summer day. The dam, bathhouse, and picnic area were built in the 1930s by the Civilian Conservation Corps. These impressive structures are among the finest examples of the many beautiful recreational facilities built by the CCC in the 1930s.

A stone and concrete footbridge crosses the pool's upper end. You can also cross Walnut Creek below the dam on stone steps leading to Charlton's amphitheater. Just downstream from the amphitheater and dam are individual picnic sites overlooking the creek and pool. Wooden decks bordering the swimming hole next to the dam are perfect for lounging and for dangling your feet in the water, and the grassy slope west of Walnut Creek is a wonderful spot for sunbathing.

The campground at Charlton is divided into three loops. Loop A is on the hilltop west of the swimming hole. Its sites are shady and have level tent pads. Some sites on the outside of the loop are not very spacious. A bathhouse in the center of the loop has flush toilets and cold showers. Loop A is a pretty camp area, but its drawback is highway noise from nearby US 270.

CAMPGROUND RATINGS

Beauty: ★★★★★
Site privacy: ★★★
Site spaciousness: ★★★★
Quiet: ★★★★
Security: ★★★★
Cleanliness/upkeep: ★★★★★

Formed by a 1930s CCC dam on Walnut Creek, Charlton's picturesque swimming hole is a perfect antidote for summer heat and humidity in the Ouachitas.

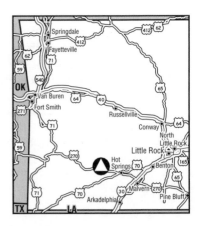

OUACHITA NATIONAL FOREST

Loop B is farther from the highway and the swimming area, so it's quieter. Sites 1–5 are beautifully shaded but not very spacious. They're jammed tightly together on a small spur off the entrance road to Loop B. Campsites 11–13 are at the back of Loop B, on the spur leading to the camp administrator's house. These spacious, level, shady, and well-spaced sites are the best spots on the loop. The remaining sites in Loop B are situated on the road encircling the bathhouse. They are all shady, level, and well spaced, but not very private.

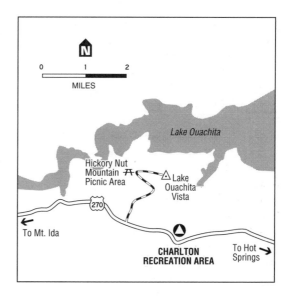

Loops A and B are the last to open in spring and the first to close as the season winds down. Loop C stays open longest and has some of the best tent sites at Charlton. It also has a brand-new bathhouse with hot showers. Sites 1–10 in Loop C are RV sites with full hookups. Luckily, the bathhouse sits between the RV sites and the tent sites. Grassy open areas surround the RV sites, so they're great for small groups needing a combination of RV and tent sites.

Sites 11–19 in Loop C are the most remote sites at Charlton. They're situated at the end of Loop C, opposite the bathhouse from the RV sites. Perched on a benchland above Walnut Creek, they are quiet, shady, and spaced about 100 feet apart. Their small parking pads and narrow campground road keep RVs and travel trailers from using this part of the camp, preserving its primitive atmosphere.

Charlton is a popular getaway from nearby Hot Springs. The RV sites usually fill up during the summer, but except for three-day weekends, you can usually find a tent site here. Charlton is a perfect camp for exploring nearby

Hot Springs National Park. If you just want to hang out in camp, the swimming hole is a cool treat on a hot day. A 0.8-mile interpretive trail explores the hillside between Loops A and B, and interpretive programs are held in the amphitheater every Saturday evening between Memorial Day and Labor Day weekends.

A nearby attraction worth a look is Hickory Nut Mountain. It's only a few miles from Charlton on a gravel road leading to a mountaintop above Lake Ouachita. It used to be a scenic highland campground, but now it's open only for picnicking. Keep going past the picnic area to the overlook on the narrow ridgetop at the end of the road. It has one of the best vistas of Lake Ouachita and its surrounding mountains, and it's a great place to watch the sunrise over the lake.

If you're feeling a little more active, put on your hiking boots or jump onto your mountain bike and take off on the Charlton Trail. It leaves the recreation area on the far side of the dam and switchbacks up the hillside above the swimming hole, then meanders 4 miles to Crystal Springs Recreation Area on Lake Ouachita. Along the way it crosses two ridges with scenic vistas of the surrounding countryside. This single-track trail is not technical, but long climbs might make it tough for novice mountain bikers.

If you run out of things to do at Charlton, check out Lake Ouachita. There you can rent a boat to go water-skiing, fishing, or sightseeing on this grand expanse of blue water in the Ouachita Mountains.

To get there: Take US 270 20 miles west of Hot Springs.

KEY INFORMATION

Charlton Recreation Area
Ouachita National Forest
P.O. Box 255,
US Highway 270 E.
Mt. Ida, AR 71957

Operated by: U.S. Forest Service

Information: (870) 867-2101

Open: April 14–November 27

Individual sites: 55 single, 2 double, 2 group

Each site has: Table, fire pit with grate, lantern pole; some sites have tent pads and barbecue grills; sites 1–10 in Loop C have full hookups

Site assignment: First come, first served

Registration: Self-pay at campground entrance

Facilities: Water, flush toilets, showers, swimming hole, picnic area, pavilion, playground, amphitheater, dump station, phone, trail

Parking: At individual site

Fee: $10 single, $20 double, $16 sites with hookups, $3 per vehicle for day-use areas

Elevation: 675 feet

Restrictions:

Pets—Allowed on leash

Fires—In fire pits

Alcoholic beverages—At site only

Vehicles—Up to 35 feet

Other—14-day stay limit; no fishing or glass containers in swimming hole

DRAGOVER

Sims, AR

Dragover is a beautiful, quiet campground hidden away on a horseshoe bend of the scenic Ouachita River. The river is only a few feet downhill from the campsites, with a forested mountainside rising steeply from the opposite shore. The Ouachita River is great for tubing, canoeing, and fishing. A calm and quiet atmosphere makes this Ouachita hideaway an excellent place to settle into camp with a cold beverage and to watch the river flow quietly past your site.

Several of Dragover's beautifully landscaped campsites are terraced into the hillside above the Ouachita River. Situated on a benchland overlooking the water, all sites are shady and have level tent pads. Most sites are well separated from their neighbors, and all have great views of the river. Sites 6 and 7 at the north end of the campground are close together, but site 7 is still the pick camping spot at Dragover. It's on a ledge overlooking the Ouachita, with a pole fence on two sides to keep you from falling off the benchland. It has especially nice views in winter, when the trees are bare of leaves.

Unless you just come to Dragover to read and relax, water sports are the attraction at this campground. A staircase descends from the campsites to a deep hole in the Ouachita, perfect for wading, swimming, or lazing in the sun. The Ouachita is a nice float stream, too. Over its 70-mile length it passes tall mountains, craggy bluffs, deep pools, and numerous riffles and rapids in its upper

CAMPGROUND RATINGS

Beauty: ★★★★★
Site privacy: ★★★
Site spaciousness: ★★★
Quiet: ★★★★
Security: ★★★★
Cleanliness/upkeep: ★★★★★

A long horseshoe bend in the Ouachita River makes Dragover float camp the perfect campground for self-shuttled river exploration

OUACHITA NATIONAL FOREST

reaches. It is not as crowded as more popular rivers in northwest Arkansas—when the Buffalo, Mulberry, and Big Piney are bank-to-bank with canoes, you can still enjoy a peaceful drift down the Ouachita.

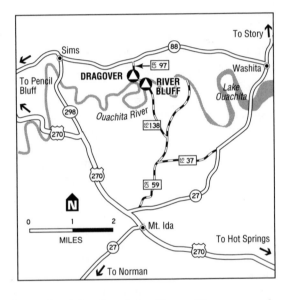

The calm flows and deep pools of the lower river make it a great float for families. From Rocky Shoals to Dragover it's a nice 9-mile, one-day trip. The most popular float runs from Oden to Rocky Shoals, where several rapids and a towering bluff several miles before the take-out make this a beautiful 10-mile reach of the Ouachita. If you like your paddling trips flat and slow, canoe the 11 miles from Dragover's river access into Lake Ouachita, finishing your trip at the Highway 27 Recreation Area.

Dragover is unique, because you can do a two-hour float without a shuttle. The campground is on the neck of a long horseshoe bend in the Ouachita. From where you turn into the campground, Dragover Road becomes a narrow forest track and meanders across the neck to a dead end at the other side of the horseshoe bend. Starting from camp, you can float for two hours, covering several quiet backcountry river miles, to a take-out that's only a 10-minute walk from camp and your car. This stretch is a wonderful tubing run, though a bit long for small children.

Bring your fishing gear to Dragover, too—the Ouachita is an excellent fishing stream. In the river's depths you'll hook catfish and spotted, smallmouth, and largemouth bass. Since most of the river is inaccessible, except by boat, Dragover is a perfect base for striking out via canoe to hook the river's fish populations.

For hikers and mountain bikers, Dragover is only a short drive from two trailheads on the 37-mile Womble Trail. This beautiful path through the

Ouachita National Forest is one of the state's prettiest trails and is considered by mountain bikers to be the best ride in the state. The AR 298 trailhead is only a few miles to the west, and several miles east the trail crosses AR 88.

The eastern part of the trail is seldom visited, but offers excellent hiking and biking. Between AR 27 and AR 88, it crosses several streams, passes through deep forests, and climbs to a knifelike ridge with spectacular views of the upper end of Lake Ouachita. Below one of the bluffs is a rope swing for splashing into the lake. Continuing west from AR 27, you'll be treated to still more beautiful vistas of the lake.

This Womble Trail is a mountain biker's dream. Seldom does a single-track trail cover such rugged and beautiful terrain while still being relatively easy to ride. It's a great place for beginners to get that first taste of single-track. Even novices will rarely have to portage on this well-designed and well-constructed trail. The main challenges are the climbs and descents between the hills and hollows along the Womble. Switchbacks keep the ascents manageable, but long climbs require riders to be in good condition.

By using forest roads you can create several good mountain bike loops in the Ouachita National Forest near Dragover. Pick up a map of the national forest from offices in nearby Mt. Ida or Oden, settle into camp at Dragover, and have a blast biking, hiking, or canoeing.

To get there: From Pencil Bluff, drive 7 miles east on AR 88 to CR 97/Dragover Road. Turn south and drive 1 mile to the campground.

KEY INFORMATION

Dragover Float Camp
Ouachita National Forest
P.O. Box 332,
    AR Highway 88 W.
Oden, AR 71961

Operated by: U.S. Forest Service

Information: (870) 326-4322

Open: Year-round

Individual sites: 7

Each site has: Table, fire pit with grate, lantern pole, tent pad

Site assignment: First come, first served

Registration: Self-pay at campground entrance

Facilities: Vault toilets, river access

Parking: At individual site

Fee: $7 per site, $3 per car for day-use

Elevation: 640 feet

Restrictions:

Pets—Allowed on leash

Fires—In fire pits

Alcoholic beverages—At site only

Vehicles—Up to 30 feet

Other—14-day stay limit; no glass containers in river

MILL CREEK

Y City, AR

T his campground is an undiscovered and seldom-visited jewel in the Ouachita National Forest. Folks just don't come here, and I think they're really missing out. Situated in the deep valley between the long ridges of Mill Creek Mountain to the north and Fourche Mountain to the south, Mill Creek Recreation Area is a quiet hideaway in a stately grove of oaks and pines.

These trees make every site a shady one at Mill Creek. The rare combination of light visitation and good spacing makes camping here a joy. Each site is screened from its neighbors by the woods, and all are level and spacious. Mill Creek's 15 campsites are scattered along a paved campground road paralleling the stream. The sites north of the road are only a few steps from Mill Creek. The muted roar of Mill Creek tumbling over rocks and ledges in its course through the forest will lull you to sleep.

Mill Creek is a great place to hang out. The shady campsites next to the stream are wonderful places to relax, read, nap, or shoot the breeze with your companions. If the shade isn't cool enough for you, walk to the east end of the camp. There the creek has been dammed to form a 12-foot deep swimming hole. Overlooked by a low bluff to the north, this pool is perfect for a cooling dip on a hot summer day.

If you want to get warmed up before your swim, take a hike on the two short trails at Mill Creek. From the south side of the picnic

CAMPGROUND RATINGS

Beauty: ★★★★
Site privacy: ★★★★★
Site spaciousness: ★★★★★
Quiet: ★★★★
Security: ★★★★
Cleanliness/upkeep: ★★★★★

At Mill Creek you can follow your mountain bike ride on the Fourche Mountain Trail with a cooling splash in the campground's swimming hole.

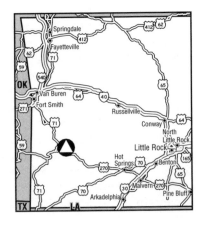

OUACHITA NATIONAL FOREST

area the Trestle Trail meanders 1 mile through the forest next to the creek. At the eastern end of the picnic area, the 0.9-mile Homestead Trail follows an interpretive loop with a spur leading to a scenic overlook of Mill Creek.

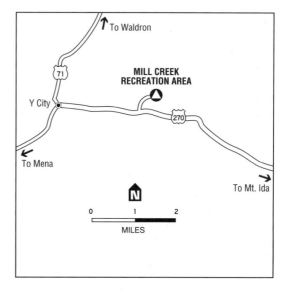

To really work up a sweat for that swim, take off south from the pay station on the Fourche Mountain Trail. It's a 27-mile network of trails with varying degrees of difficulty, all open to hikers, mountain bikers, and equestrians. Numbered posts at each intersection correspond to markers on the trail map available from the forest service. Distances and difficulty ratings of segments between intersections are noted on the map, letting you choose on your hike or ride distances and challenge levels you like. This network follows a combination of old roads, faded double-track, and newly cut single-track.

Fourche Mountain is a typical miles-long ridge in the Ouachita Mountain range. The trail system covers a patch of mountainside about 4 miles wide and 5 miles long, with a scenic high point at Buck Knob in the southeast corner of the network. Several creeks tumble down the mountainside in spring, and beautiful rock walls overlook Rock Creek on the network's eastern perimeter. My favorite spot is high on the west side of the trail system near intersection 2, where two streams come together to form the headwaters of Turner Creek. You'll splash through both these creeks on a rock ledge—a perfect place to dangle your feet in the stream.

Hikers will like all trails in the system, but some of these paths on Fourche Mountain are difficult for mountain bikers. The trail segments between intersection points 1 and 10 and points 3 and 9 are difficult, even for experts. If you don't mind pedaling extra miles in return for an easier route, ride up to the south side of the trail system on roads. Once there, you can enjoy long trail descents back to Mill Creek Recreation Area. To do this, ride US 270 7 miles east to Forest Road 76. Turn right on FS 76 and follow it 5 miles to intersect the trail system near the FS 76/FS 76A junction. From there, either ride down the east side of the system along Rock Creek, or follow the Ouachita Trail 5 miles east to the western perimeter of the network.

The south side of the Fourche Mountain Trail connects to the Ouachita National Recreation Trail, a 223-mile jaunt from Talimena State Park in Oklahoma to Pinnacle Mountain State Park near Little Rock. This scenic trail follows ridgetops for miles and miles, with spectacular views of the Ouachita Mountains, especially when the trees are bare of leaves. Good access points for hiking the Ouachita near Mill Creek are Big Brushy Campground to the east on US 270, Foran Gap Trailhead on US 71 south of Y City, and FS 76 on the south side of the Fourche Mountain Trail.

For detailed information on the Fourche Mountain Trail and the Ouachita National Recreation Trail, pick up copies of *Mountain Bike! The Ozarks* by Steven Henry, the Ouachita Trail Guide by Tim Ernst (see the Bibliography on page 168), and a map of the Ouachita National Forest. These guides will clue you in to what's out there around Mill Creek and keep you on the trail.

To get there: Take US 270 30 miles west of Mt. Ida or 5 miles east of Y City. Mill Creek is on the north side of US 270.

KEY INFORMATION

**Mill Creek Recreation Area
Ouachita National Forest
P.O. Box 2255, US 71 and
AR 248
Waldron, AR 72958**

Operated by: U.S. Forest Service

Information: (501) 637-4174

Open: April 10–September 5

Individual sites: 15

Each site has: Table, fire pit with grate, lantern pole, tent pad

Site assignment: First come, first served

Registration: Self-pay at campground entrance

Facilities: Water, flush toilets, swimming hole, picnic area, trails

Parking: At individual site

Fee: $5 per site, $3 per vehicle for day-use area

Elevation: 880 feet

Restrictions:

Pets—Allowed on leash

Fires—In fire pits

Alcoholic beverages—At site only

Vehicles—Up to 28 feet

Other—14-day stay limit; no glass containers in swimming area; no fishing in swimming hole

RIVER BLUFF

Mt. Ida, AR

Some folks might fear getting bored at River Bluff Float Camp where there aren't the myriad activities and attractions offered at places like Albert Pike and Devil's Den. Not me—I think this semi-primitive campground is what tent camping is all about. This quiet, end-of-the-road getaway is a wonderful place to read, write, nap, or laze in your lawn chair on the gravel bar. A thick canopy of trees keeps the camp nice and cool. If you do get a little warm, a dip in the Ouachita River is only a few steps away. A craggy bluff rises above camp on the other side of the Ouachita, overlooking the swimming hole and shoals in the river next to camp. You can also fish and canoe in the Ouachita, and a spur trail leads to the Womble Trail.

There are only seven unnumbered sites at this laid-back hideaway in a wide bend of the Ouachita River. A loop road circles this campground situated on a low bench above the stream. Four very nice sites overlook the river. Across from those are two sites on the inside of the loop. My favorite spot is the last one, a secluded campsite set back into the trees at the end of the loop drive. All sites are spacious and well shaded, but this one is the roomiest and most private of all.

The Ouachita is a nice float stream, made all the better by not being as well known as the float streams up north. On weekends when the Buffalo, Big Piney, Mulberry, or

CAMPGROUND RATINGS

Beauty:	★★★★★
Site privacy:	★★★★★
Site spaciousness:	★★★★★
Quiet:	★★★★★
Security:	★★★★
Cleanliness/upkeep:	★★★

River Bluff is a peaceful end-of-the-road hideaway next to the Ouachita River.

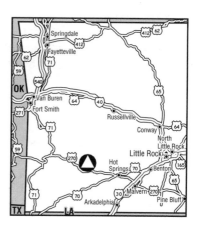

OUACHITA NATIONAL FOREST

other famous Ozark water-
ways are crowded and crazy,
you can enjoy solitude on a
peaceful canoe trip down the
Ouachita. It's a 5-mile float
from Fulton Branch to River
Bluff and 12 miles from
Rocky Shoals.

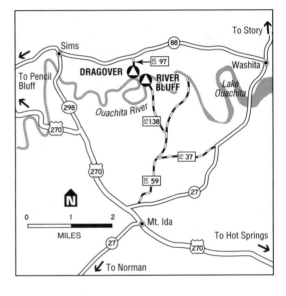

While water levels are opti-
mal March–early June, the
river around River Bluff is
usually floatable year-round.
Although dry seasons might
mean dragging your canoe
over a few shallows, you'll be
drifting through clear waters
most of the way. While paddling the Ouachita you'll see
blue herons, kingfishers, deer, beaver, deep pools, and sparkling shoals. Bring
your fishing gear with you—the Ouachita supports populations of small and
largemouth bass, spotted and rock bass, sunfish, catfish, and bluegill.

Bring your hiking shoes and mountain bike when you come to River Bluff.
The 37-mile Womble Trail, considered by many to be the best mountain bike
ride in Arkansas, passes close to camp. The designers did a superb job on this
trail, using switchbacks to keep the grade easy; the trail surface has few rocky
and technical stretches. It's a great ride for novices to enjoy their first single-
track experience. Rarely will you find a trail that traverses such rugged terrain
and is still relatively easy to pedal. The Womble follows ridgetops for miles,
swooping around the upper reaches of hollows that contain tributaries of the
Ouachita. Fast, smooth descents are followed by long, gradual climbs to the
top of the next ridge. Scenic views are everywhere. They are especially
impressive in winter, when leaves are off the trees.

A 1.6-mile spur trail leads from River Bluff to the Womble Trail. From there
you can put together nice trail-road loop combinations through the national

forest. It's a fairly easy trail ride 4 miles west to Fulton Branch Float Camp. From Fulton Branch, return to River Bluff on little-traveled County Roads 61 and 59 and FS 138 to finish a 12-mile loop. Riding the Womble 5 miles east from the trail junction is harder but much more scenic. As you approach AR 27, you'll climb gradually to several beautiful vistas over an arm of Lake Ouachita, then make a fast, smooth descent to the AR 27 trailhead. From there take AR 27, FS 37, CR 59, and FS 138 back to River Bluff for a great 16-mile loop. Bring maps of the Ouachita National Forest and the Womble Trail with you, and you'll have no problem finding your way through the forest.

River Bluff Recreation Area is a wonderful place—laid-back, beautiful, and free. It's one of the last good deals in the outdoors, but it comes with a price—no water in the campground and no trash pickup. Bring your water in and take your trash out. When I've camped at River Bluff it's been beautiful and clean, but others have told me they've seen the place look pretty sloppy. Be a friend of this comfortable riverside hideaway— take your own trash out plus a little more, leaving River Bluff better than you found it.

To get there: Drive a half mile north from Mt. Ida on AR 27 to County Road 59. Turn left and drive northwest 3.5 miles on CR 59 to Forest Road 138. Turn left on FS 138 and drive 3 miles to the camp. Most intersections will have signs to guide you.

KEY INFORMATION

**River Bluff Float Camp
Ouachita National Forest
P.O. Box 255, Highway 270 E.
Mt. Ida, AR 71957**

Operated by: U.S. Forest Service

Information: (870) 867-2101

Open: Year-round

Individual sites: 7

Each site has: Table, fire pit with grate, lantern pole

Site assignment: First come, first served

Registration: No registration required

Facilities: Vault toilets, river access, trail

Parking: At individual site

Fee: No fee

Elevation: 630 feet

Restrictions:

Pets—Allowed on leash

Fires—In fire pits

Alcoholic beverages—Allowed, subject to local ordinances

Vehicles—Up to 20 feet

Other—14-night stay limit; no glass containers in river

SHADY LAKE

Athens, AR

S hady Lake Recreation Area, one of many Civilian Conservation Corps projects built in Arkansas in the 1930s, is a sparkling-blue jewel nestled at the base of Tall Peak. The campground is hidden in a grove of tall pines and hardwoods next to a 25-acre lake surrounded by forested mountains. A rambling CCC-constructed bathhouse overlooks the beach and its diving platform a few feet above the deep blue water. Two trails leave right from the campground, and 50 miles of additional hiking and mountain biking trails are within 10 miles of Shady Lake.

Driving into the recreation area, the first things you see are the bathhouse and the lake. Loop A is immediately south of the bathhouse. All sites in Loop A are well shaded and have wonderful views of the lake, but they are a little tightly packed. Loop A opens early in the season and stays open later than the other four loops.

The remaining four loops are along the road leading north from the bathhouse. Two of Loop B's 28 shady sites are on a knoll with views of the lake. Several campsites on this loop are next to the Saline River, the stream that fills Shady Lake. Loop E is on a hilltop away from the lake. It's the least attractive of the five loops. Shade is good there, but the ground is rocky, and many sites are too close to their neighbors. Loop E is also used as a group campground. Loop D is next to the river,

CAMPGROUND RATINGS

Beauty: ★★★★★

Site privacy: ★★★★

Site spaciousness: ★★★★★

Quiet: ★★★★

Security: ★★★★

Cleanliness/upkeep: ★★★★★

From beaches to mountains— at Shady Lake you can have it all.

OUACHITA NATIONAL FOREST

with five of its 15 sites being prime spots next to the stream. In Loop D shade and site spacing are excellent.

My favorite sites are in Loop C. It's away from the lake, at the far end of the recreation area, and its location gives it a comfortably remote atmosphere. Seven of its 22 sites are either next to the Saline River or on a bench overlooking the stream. Most sites are decently spaced from their neighbors, and some have beautiful stonewalled terraces between the table and

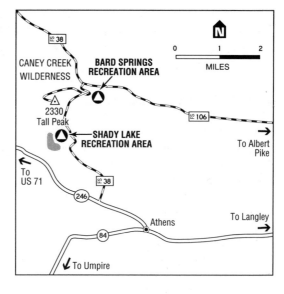

races between the table and the tent pad. Every site is heavily shaded, and you can access two trails by crossing the slab bridge behind site 1.

One of these is the 3.2-mile Shady Lake Trail. This scenic loop around the lake is open to both hikers and mountain bikers. It's a great hike or ride for all skill levels. You'll have only one long climb, and your reward will be a scenic view of the blue waters below. A highlight on the loop is at the lake's south end, where the trail fords the Saline River below the impressive CCC dam. Water cascading over the dam forms several quiet pools that reflect rugged stone formations rising above. The trail then climbs to an overlook next to the dam, where you can admire the vista of Shady Lake and Tall Peak.

After warming up on the Shady Lake Trail, hike the Tall Peak Trail from Shady Lake to the mountaintop. There you can gaze over the surrounding Ouachita Mountains from the fire lookout on the summit. If you fear the climb, have someone drive you up there, and then hike back down. It's a rough road—but my old Mazda 626 made it, so you will too. The view from 2,330-foot Tall Peak is worth whatever you have to do to get there.

The trail leaves Shady Lake behind site C-1. It's a little over 3 miles to the peak on a really nice trail. You'll follow the Saline River for a while, crossing it four times in the first mile. From the last crossing it's uphill to the peak, past rock outcroppings, scenic views, and across a portion of the Caney Creek Wilderness. The closer you get to the top, the more fantastic the views. That's why I like hiking up instead of down—the best comes at the end, rewarding my efforts. When you look back from Tall Peak and see tiny Shady Lake shimmering far below, you'll appreciate how far you've climbed!

If the hike to Tall Peak whets your appetite for more of the Caney Creek Wilderness, two trailheads on FS 38 north of Shady Lake access 15 more miles of hiking on the Caney Creek and Buckeye Trails. Another beautiful hike, the 10-mile Athens–Big Fork Trail leaves from a trailhead just southeast of Shady Lake and follows a 100-year-old postal route. The Little Missouri Trail is 14 miles past Shady Lake. This trail is a 16-mile hike or bike past Little Missouri Falls and through the incomparable Winding Stairs (see the Albert Pike profile on page 144 for more about Winding Stairs).

Before coming to Shady Lake, write the Ouachita National Forest for maps of all these trails. While you're at it, get the Ouachita National Forest map, too—it'll show you the miles and miles of scenic back roads in the Ouachita.

To get there: From Athens, drive 2.5 miles west on AR 246 to Shady Lake Road, FS 38. Turn north on FS 38 and follow it 3.75 miles to Shady Lake.

KEY INFORMATION

Shady Lake Recreation Area
Ouachita National Forest
1603 Highway 71 N.
Mena, AR 71953

Operated by: U.S. Forest Service

Information: (501) 394-2382

Open: March 1–December 4

Individual sites: 97

Each site has: Table, fire pit with grate, lantern pole; most sites have tent pads; some sites have barbecue grills and extra lantern pole; site A-7 has electricity and water; sites C-22 and B-1 have full hookups

Site assignment: First come, first served

Registration: Self-pay at campground entrance

Facilities: Flush toilets, water, showers, picnic area, pavilion, lake with beach and bathhouse, playground, volleyball court, horseshoe pits (get horseshoes from host)

Parking: At individual site

Fee: $10 single site, $16 double site, $3 per vehicle for day-use

Elevation: 1,100 feet

Restrictions:

Pets—Allowed on leash; not allowed in swimming area

Fires—In fire pits

Alcoholic beverages—At campsite only

Vehicles—Up to 30 feet at most sites; up to 60 feet at some sites

Other—14-day stay limit

APPENDICES

APPENDIX A
Camping Equipment Checklist

Except for the large and bulky items on this list, I keep a plastic storage container full of the essentials of car camping, so that they're ready to go when I am. I make a last-minute check of the inventory, resupply anything that's low or missing, and away I go!

Cooking Utensils
Bottle opener
Bottles of salt, pepper, spices, sugar,
  cooking oil, and maple syrup in
  waterproof, spillproof containers
Can opener
Corkscrew
Cups, plastic or tin
Dish soap (biodegradable), sponge,
  and towel
Flatware
Food of your choice
Frying pan
Fuel for stove
Matches in waterproof container
Plates
Pocketknife
Pot with lid
Spatula
Stove
Tin foil
Wooden spoon

First Aid Kit
Band-Aids
First aid cream
Gauze pads
Ibuprofen or aspirin
Insect repellent
Moleskin
Snakebite kit
Sunscreen/Chap Stick

Tape, waterproof adhesive

Sleeping Gear
Pillow
Sleeping bag
Sleeping pad, inflatable or insulated
Tent with ground tarp and rainfly

Miscellaneous
Bath soap (biodegradable), washcloth,
  and towel
Camp chair
Candles
Cooler
Deck of cards
Fire starter
Flashlight with fresh batteries
Foul-weather clothing
Lantern
Maps (road, topographic, trail, etc.)
Paper towels
Plastic zip-top bags
Sunglasses
Toilet paper
Water bottle

Optional
Barbecue grill
Binoculars
Canoe with paddles
Field guides on bird, plant, and
  wildlife identification
Fishing rod and tackle

APPENDIX B
Suggested Reading and Reference

Ernst, Tim. *Arkansas Hiking Trails: A Guide to Seventy-Eight Selected Trails in the Natural State.* 2d ed. Wilderness Visions Press, 1994.

Ernst, Tim. *Buffalo River Hiking Trails.* Wilderness Visions Press, 1998.

Ernst, Tim. *Ouachita Trail Guide.* 3d ed. CLOUDLAND.NET, 2000.

Ernst, Tim. *Ozark Highlands Trail Guide.* 4th ed. CLOUDLAND.NET, 1998.

Frey, Kelly, and Steve Baron. *Trails of Missouri--A Guide to Hiking the Show-Me State.* Steve Baron, 1995.

Gass, Ramon. *Missouri Hiking Trails: A Detailed Guide to Selected Hiking Trails of Public Land in Missouri.* Missouri Department of Conservation, 1996.

Hawksley, Oz. *Missouri Ozark Waterways.* Missouri Department of Conservation, 1965.

Hendricks, Bryan. *Arkansas: A Guide to Backcountry Travel & Adventure.* Out There Press, 1999.

Henry, Steve. *Mountain Bike! The Ozarks A Guide to the Classic Trails.* 2d ed. Menasha Ridge Press, 2000.

Knight, Theresa. *Conservation Trails: A Guide to Missouri Department of Conservation Hiking Trails.* Missouri Department of Conservation, 1999.

McPherson, Alan. *One Hundred Nature Walks in the Missouri Ozarks.* Cache River Press, 1997.

Tryon, Chuck, and Sharon Tryon. *Fly Fishing For Trout In Missouri.* 2d ed. Ozark Mountain Fly Fishers, 1999.

INDEX

ABOUT THE AUTHOR

Steve Henry grew up on a farm in the rolling hills of central Kansas, spending much of his youth working under the blue skies of the plains. After earning Bachelor's degrees in Marketing and Agricultural Economics at Kansas State University, he served a sentence of seven years in the offices of an insurance company. Missing the outdoor life, he finally left the insurance company in 1985 to cycle across the continent twice, including one trek from Anchorage, Alaska, to Key West, Florida. Since then he has organized triathlons, led bicycle and backpack tours, written articles for Cycle St. Louis (a local bicycling publication), and enjoyed many camping trips. Steve is also the author of *Mountain Bike! The Ozarks* (Menasha Ridge Press). "The best thing about writing this guide was discovering the beauty of the Ozarks," says Steve. "I knew Missouri was beautiful, but Arkansas was a pleasant surprise to me. It's one of the best-kept secrets in the country."